THE CARIBOO MISSION

A History of the Oblates

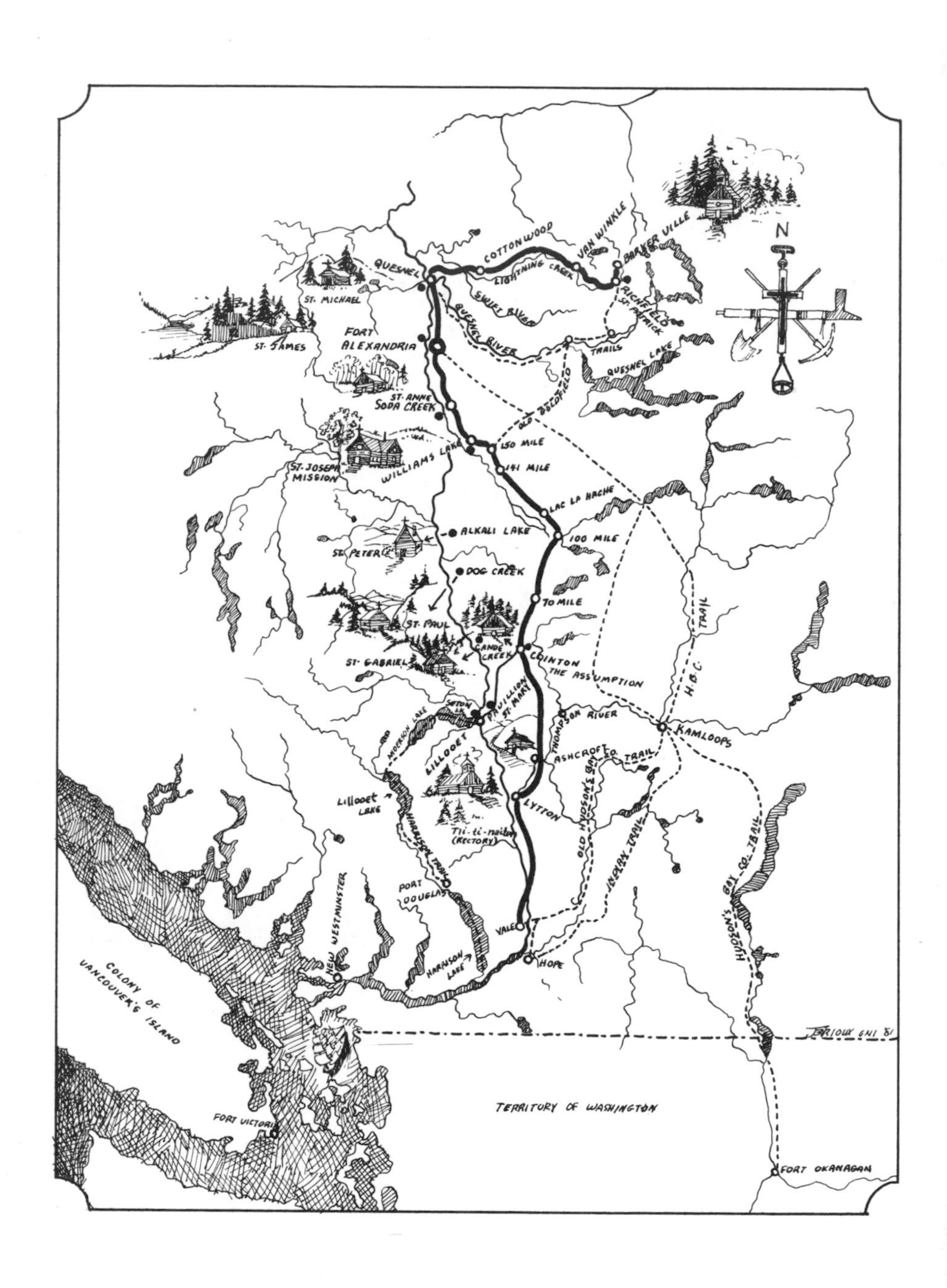
N
QUESNEL
COTTONWOOD
VAN WINKLE
BARKER VILLE
LIGHTNING CREEK
SWIFT RIVER
RICHFIELD
ST. PATRICK
ST. MICHAEL
ST. JAMES
FORT ALEXANDRIA
QUESNEL RIVER
TRAILS
QUESNEL LAKE
ST. ANNE
SODA CREEK
150 MILE
141 MILE
WILLIAMS LAKE
ST. JOSEPH MISSION
LAC LA HACHE
100 MILE
ALKALI LAKE
ST. PETER
DOG CREEK
70 MILE
ST. PAUL
CANOE CREEK
CLINTON
THE ASSUMPTION
ST. GABRIEL
H.B.C. TRAIL
SETON LK.
PAVILLION
ST. MARY
THOMPSON RIVER
KAMLOOPS
ANDERSON LAKE
LILLOOET
ASHCROFT
HUDSON'S BAY CO. TRAIL
Lillooet Lake
LYTTON
OLD HUDSON'S BAY CO. TRAIL
INDIAN TRAIL
HARRISON TRAIL
(RECTORY)
PORT DOUGLAS
NEW WESTMINSTER
VALE
HOPE
HARRISON LAKE
COLONY OF VANCOUVER'S ISLAND
TERRITORY OF WASHINGTON
FORT VICTORIA
FORT OKANAGAN

THE CARIBOO MISSION

A History of the Oblates

MARGARET
WHITEHEAD

1981
Sono Nis Press
Victoria, British Columbia, Canada

Canadian Cataloguing in Publication Data

Whitehead, Margaret Mary, 1937-
The Cariboo Mission

Bibliography; p.

Includes index
ISBN 0-919462-91-x

1. Cariboo Mission — History. 2. Oblates of Mary Immaculate — Missions — British Columbia — History. 3. Catholic Church — Missions — British Columbia — History. 4. Indians of North America — Missions — British Columbia — History.

I. Title
BV2300.02W49 266'.27112 C81-091272-4

First Printing July 1981
Second Printing January 1982

Published by
SONO NIS PRESS
1745 Blanshard Street
Victoria, British Columbia v8w 2J8

Designed and printed in Canada by
MORRISS PRINTING COMPANY LTD.
Victoria, British Columbia

For my husband Alan
and my friend Orland O'Regan, O.M.I.

CONTENTS

9 *Preface*

11 CHAPTER I "Behold, a New Mission"

27 CHAPTER II The People and Religion

41 CHAPTER III "Thc Brightest Hopes"

55 CHAPTER IV Missionaries to Ranchers

66 CHAPTER V A New Direction

79 CHAPTER VI "Too Many Irons in the Fire"

93 CHAPTER VII "The Golden Age"

109 CHAPTER VIII "The Mission"

130 CHAPTER IX A New Era

137 *Index*

Acknowledgements

I wish to thank my husband Alan for his constant support and assistance with research, the Oblate Community, particularly former and present missionaries to the Cariboo whose important work I frequently interrupted, the Indian people of the Cariboo who welcomed and informed me, John Brioux, O.M.I. for his excellent illustrations, and Dr. Patricia Roy, Dr. Brian Dippie, and Dr. Michael Hadley who offered perceptive observations, constructive criticism, and sound advice.

Archives Abbreviations

Archives of the Archdiocese of Quebec:	A.A.Q.
Archives generales, Rome:	A.G. Rome
Archives Deschâtelets:	A.D.
Archives of the Sisters of St. Ann, Lachine:	A.S.S.A., Lachine
Archives of the Sisters of St. Ann, Victoria:	A.S.S.A., Victoria
Oblate Archives, Vancouver	O.A.
Provincial Archives of British Columbia:	P.A.B.C.

PREFACE

Maps of British Columbia indicate by a red dot and a caption the position of the historical site occupied by St. Joseph's Mission in the San José Valley approximately twelve miles southwest of Williams Lake. Tourists attracted by the caption may be disappointed in the aspect of the mission. Although the setting is beautiful, St. Joseph's has none of the glamour or charm of California's numerous mission centres. A functional though scarcely beautiful large concrete building dominates the original mission site; this served for decades as the Cariboo's Indian Residential School. A few old, rather delapidated farm buildings and a small, slightly untidy cemetary where missionaries, Indians, and settlers lie buried are the only visible link with the earliest years of the mission's history. But while it may lack beauty and any of the commercial aspects frequently associated with historic sites, St. Joseph's Mission has a history as old as the earliest days of white settlement in the Cariboo.

A French order, the Oblates of Mary Immaculate, purchased the site in 1866. Their objective was to bring Catholicism to the numerous peoples of the Cariboo. Built at a time when these people were confronting a new and aggressive threat, the beginning of permanent white settlement, the Mission witnessed and participated in both the re-ordering of Indian civilization through Indian contact with a permanent white presence and the advance of white civilization as the entrepreneural "boom and bust" towns of the 1850's and 1860's gave way to stable, prosperous ranching communities. It may lack visible tourist appeal, but the Cariboo Mission has a history as rich as the history of the Cariboo itself.

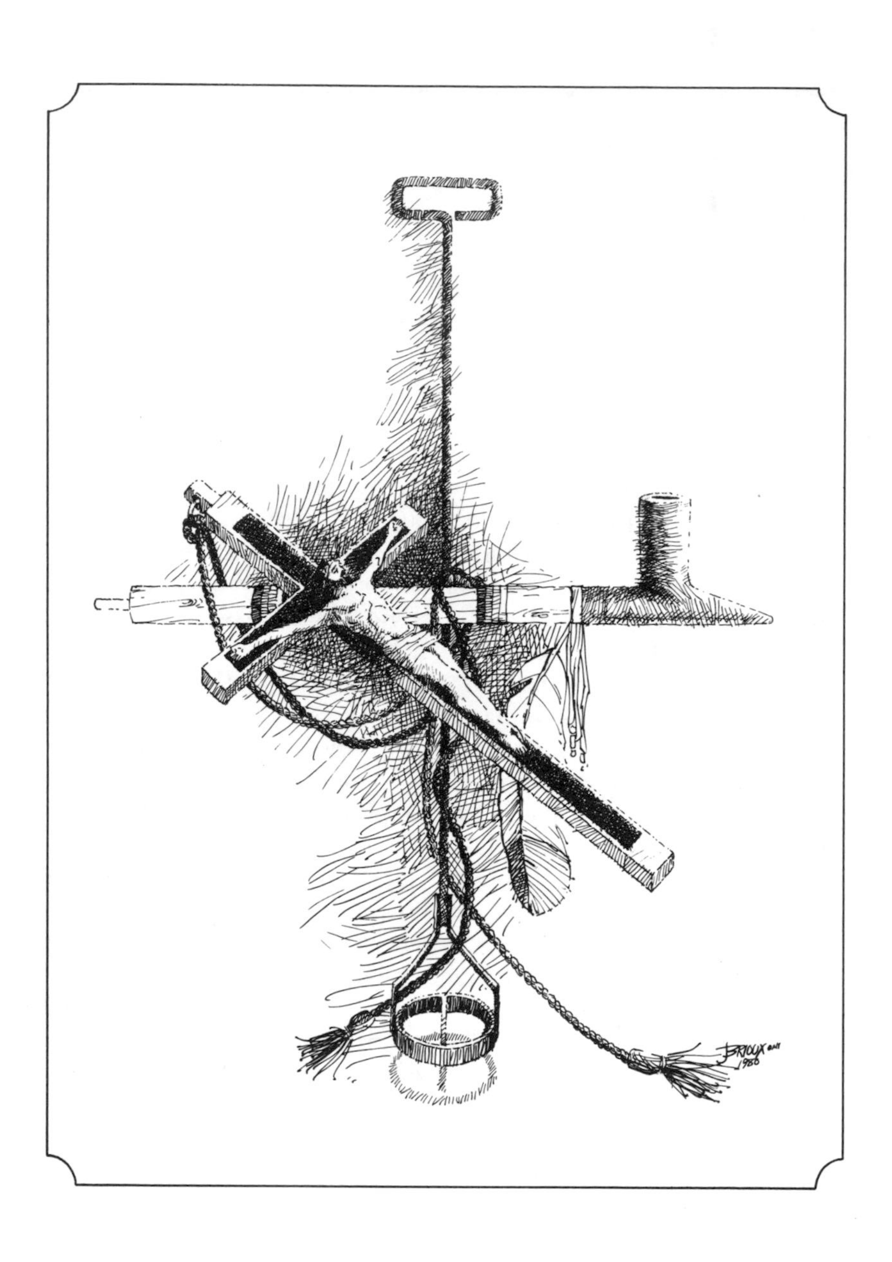

Chapter I

"BEHOLD, A NEW MISSION"

"Behold a new mission opening up before us . . . our family will preach Jesus Christ from one ocean to another in these immense regions which have never known Him; what an apostolate."[1] So wrote Eugene de Mazenod, founder of the Oblates of Mary Immaculate as his order accepted the Oregon Missions. On January 2, 1847, the first Oblate missionaries to the Pacific Coast, Father Pascal Ricard (Superior), scholastic brothers Casimir Chirouse, Charles John Felix Pandosy, Georges Blanchet and lay Brother Celestin Verney, arrived at Walla Walla, Oregon Territory, where they established St. Rose Mission on land provided, "somewhat reluctantly," by Piopiomosmos, a Walla Walla chief.[2] De Mazenod had every reason to be optimistic about the future work of his order on the West Coast. The Oblates' first foreign missionary work, begun in eastern Canada in 1842, had been so successful that the Bishop of Quebec entrusted the west also to their care.

When he founded his order in 1812, Eugene de Mazenod, a former French nobleman who had become a Provence parish priest, had little thought of missionary endeavours in foreign lands. His main concern was to provide France with worthy clergy. He deplored the fact that because of the upheavals of the French Revolution and the anti-Church policies of Napoleon, there were few men of real ability among the priests and religious orders of France; "the poorest, the most miserable, the most abject in society" were charged with bringing religious teaching to the people. When on January 25, 1816, de Mazenod inaugurated the "Missionary Society of Provence," he sought to improve both the quality of priests and religious instruction. The original statutes of the order clearly stated that the aim of the society was not only to work towards the salvation of others by devotion to the ministry of preaching but also "above all else" to provide its members with the means of practising religious virtues. Their life was to be devoted to prayer, meditation, practise of religious virtues, scripture, study of papal writing, dogmatic and moral theology, preaching to the poor, and the instruction of youth.[3] The emphasis was on self-spiritual regeneration; practical work came second. On February 17, 1826, Pope Leo XII approved the Society and the founder changed its name to the Oblates of the Most Holy and Immaculate Virgin Mary.

De Mazenod's men were to be an élite group. Writing to a would-be recruit, Father François-Henri Tempier, curate at Arles, Father de Mazenod explained that the new order would be small because he wanted men who had "the will-power and courage to walk in the footsteps of the Apostles." He described his difficulty in finding such men:

> If it were only a matter of going to preach the word of God in a haphazard fashion mixed with much human alloy or of scouring the countryside in the hope of winning souls to God without trying too hard to be really interior men, truly apostolic men, it would not be difficult . . . but do you actually think that I want this kind of merchandize? We must be truly saints ourselves.[4]

In order that they might achieve this state of perfection, the Oblates were given rules that were worthy of contemplative orders whose lives were spent in prayer. Each day's activity included periods of mental prayer, scripture study, visits to chapel, recitation of the rosary, examination of conscience and "Divine Office" (which could, in exceptional circumstances, be modified but never omitted). There were weekly and monthly retreats and spiritual conferences and, whenever possible, the Oblates were to study literature. Confronted with anti-clerical young people "writing so well, with so much skill and talent in support of lies and deceptions" de Mazenod was determined that his Oblates must also arm themselves "for this type of combat."[5] There was no excuse for omission of any of these activities.

Initially the only practical objective of the Order was to preach to the poor in the form of "missions." A "mission" consisted of a set formula of prayer and preaching over a number of weeks, concentrated on the basic tenets of the Catholic faith. De Mazenod considered this work to be the "most efficacious in the regeneration of Christianity among the people." Over the years as the community grew, the Oblates went to work among the poor in England, Ireland, and Scotland, as well as in other parts of France. When, in June 1841, Monseignor Ignace Bourget, Bishop of Montreal, stopped at Marseilles en route to Rome and requested Oblates for the preaching of missions and for tending, when required, to missions among the Indians, de Mazenod was able to oblige him. On December 2nd, 1841, the first Oblates arrived in the diocese of Quebec; three years later three Oblate missionaries were sent among the Indians of the Upper Ottawa, the Upper Saint-Maurice, the Lake St. John district and along the north shore of the Gulf of St. Lawrence. By 1845, they were established in the Red River area.

When he sanctioned this move to missionary work among the native peoples, Father de Mazenod added a new section to the Order's *Constitution and Rules*. Far from absolving the missionary Oblates from their spiritual routines, the new section stressed that difficulties presented by missionary work were no excuse for the neglect of spiritual exercises. By virtue of their removal from a congregation of Oblates, the "in-the-field" missionaries were expected to be even stricter in observing all points of the Rules, "especially those that concerned spiritual exercises."[6] Thus the small group of French missionaries arriving in Oregon in 1847 were somewhat handicapped by the inflexible time-consuming nature of their order's rules; and time was of an essence in the still young diocese of Walla Walla.

On November 24, 1838, two French Canadian Roman Catholic priests, Francis Norbert Blanchet and Modeste Demers had arrived with the fur brigade from Red River at Fort Vancouver in Oregon territory. Their task was to establish the Catholic Church "in that part of the Diocese of Quebec situated between the Pacific Ocean and the Rocky mountains."[7] Although the territory stretched from the California boundary to Alaska and included Vancouver Island and the Queen Charlotte Islands, Bishop Signay of Quebec could only spare two men. By sending Blanchet and Demers the Bishop was responding to the requests of white Catholic settlers in the Willamette Valley for priests to live among them. But Signay clearly stated that the prime objective of their mission was to Christianize the numerous Indian peoples living in the diocese.[8]

Blanchet and Demers faced two immediate challenges: limited manpower in a vast territory almost entirely inhabited by Indians and the presence of denominational rivalry in the form of established Methodist and Presbyterian missionaries. What had begun with the Reformation could not be escaped even in the still wilderness areas of the Pacific Northwest. It was as essential for the Catholic priests to save the Indians from the heresy of Protestantism as it was to save them from paganism. And although, as Blanchet wrote,[9] it was enough for the two new missionaries to hear that "some false prophet" intended visiting or establishing in a particular area to induce the priests to go there immediately, they were clearly outnumbered by other denominations and could not hope to cover all areas themselves. In order to overcome both difficulties, Father Blanchet and Father Demers had to depend on lay assistants.

At first these were appointed among the white settlers of the Willamette Valley and Blanchet assigned Mr. Fagnant, a farmer, and Peter Jacquet, an ex-sailor, to teach prayers and catechism. Then, an ingenious idea provided the missionaries with more catechists than they had hoped for. While searching for a way of giving the Indians a "plain and simple" idea of religion, Blanchet created a teaching aid that the Indians, who referred to God as "Sahale Tai," One Above, called the Sahale Stick. The device resembled a miniature totem. Blanchet took a squared stick, of a portable length, on which he represented the forty centuries before the birth of Jesus by forty linear marks, the thirty-three years of Jesus' life by thirty dots followed by a cross, and the eighteen centuries and thirty-nine years since the death of Jesus by eighteen linear marks and thirty-nine dots.[10] In this way, Blanchet was able to point to the creation, biblical events, the promise and birth of a saviour, his death, and the mission of the apostles and the Catholic missionaries. The carving became popular with the Indians, so much so that a simpler version, a chart which became known as the Catholic Ladder, replaced it.[11] These charts were distributed to chiefs willing to act as catechists among their people. In this way, many Indians learnt the Catholic missionaries' message long before they actually saw the priests. The missionaries considered the Ladder an effective means of undermining the work of their Protestant rivals.

The natural rivalry between the denominations intensified both with the use of the Catholic Ladder — a branch leading from the straight road to heaven, at the century of the Reformation, depicted the error of following Protestantism — and with the arrival of more Catholic clergy. Until 1842, with the exception of a visit by Father Peter John De Smet who with two companions was conducting missionary work among the Flatheads immediately west of the Rocky Mountains, the two French Canadian missionaries worked their vast territory alone. On September 17, 1842, Fathers Langlois and Bolduc arrived at Fort Vancouver from Canada via Cape Horn. According to the Governor of the Hudson's Bay Company Sir George Simpson, the priests had been refused passage across Canada in the canoes of the Company because of the objections of Reverend Herbert Beaver, Anglican chaplain at Fort Vancouver; because of religious rivalry, the priests were forced to travel by sea.[12]

In 1843, Rome proclaimed the missionary territory a Vicariate Apostolic the first step in creating organized ecclesiastical units in the new territory. Blanchet was appointed Vicar General with the title Bishop of Drasa. Eight months later Father De Smet, who had been seeking recruits in Europe, arrived at Fort Vancouver with four Jesuits — Fathers Ravalli, Accolti, Vercruisse, and Nobili — some lay brothers and six Sisters of Notre Dame of Namur. Over the next two years several other priests volunteered to work in the Vicariate which, on July 24, 1846, was erected into an ecclesiastical province and divided into three dioceses: Oregon City under the direction of the newly appointed Archbishop Blanchet; Vancouver Island and New Caledonia under the direction of Demers, who was elevated to Bishop, and Walla Walla (later Nisqually) which was placed under the direction of Bishop Magloire Blanchet, brother of Oregon's missionary and a former canon of Montreal cathedral who had been imprisoned for alleged activities in the Papineau Rebellion (although no charges were proved against him).[13]

The firm establishment of the Catholic Church in Oregon territory intensified denominational rivalry and, upon their arrival, the Oblates were caught up in an unsettled situation. The conflict between Catholics and Protestants became more serious when a month after the Oblates opened St. Rose Mission, minister and missionary Dr. Marcus Whitman and his wife were among a number of Americans killed by Cayuse Indians at the Presbyterian mission near Walla Walla. A second Presbyterian missionary, Reverend Henry Spalding, who had accompanied the Whitmans to Oregon and who ran a mission at Colville, accused the Catholic clergy of inciting the massacre. His accusations aroused the resentment of the rapidly increasing American settlers towards the Catholic clergy and missionaries; a resentment which must have intensified when Archbishop Blanchet visited, instructed, and baptized five Cayuse Indians several days before they were executed for their part in the attack.

This unhappy sequence of events presaged the troubled years the Oblates were to spend in Oregon. Initially Bishop Blanchet sent them to minister to the Indians of central and western present day Washington, including all the Indians of the Puget Sound area. Although in 1850 a second group of Oblates appointed to the Oregon country, one priest, Father Louis D'herbomez and two lay Brothers, Phillippe Surel and Gaspàrd Janin, arrived at Olympia, the Oblates were still pitifully few in number. In order to maintain continuity in their instruction, the missionaries often travelled with the Indians but they founded several permanent missions: St. Joseph's, Olympia (where white settlers also attended); Immaculate Conception in the land of Tiaies, and St. Joseph's of Simcoe in the land of Kamiakin (both chiefs among the Yakima); mission posts at Alachicas, on the left bank of the Yakima river, and at Ahtanum in Kamiakin's territory. The constant journeying, accidents, and malnutrition began to take their toll, and in 1853, de Mazenod, appalled by the hardships the Oblates had encountered, decided to recall them to France. Only the persuasion of the Sacred Propaganda in Rome changed his mind.[14]

To improve the situation, in November 1854, he dispatched two new priests Paul Durieu and Pierre Richard, but missionary work was not destined to progress smoothly. The outbreak of the Yakima War in 1855 caused further antagonism towards the Oblates because Chief Kamiakin, an organizer of the Indian revolt against unjust land treaties, had become a close friend of the missionaries. They were condemned by whites because they chose in spite of the war to remain at their mission posts and they were threatened by Indians to whom they represented the white establishment. Added to the problems caused by this unenviable situation, were the clashes between the Oblates and the French-Canadian bishops.

In both Canon Law and the Oblate Constitution, the Oblate missionary superior and his priests had to accept the directives of Oregon's ecclesiastical leaders. However, what the Oblates felt was necessary to achieve their missionary goals and what the ecclesiastical leaders felt was imperative for the good of the entire Church in Oregon were not always compatible. Although some causes of discontent are somewhat obscure, two particular areas of grievance came to light. Land pre-empted by the Oblates for development of missions and mission farms had to be registered in the name of individual Oblates, since American law did not recognize the rights of religious groups to own communal property. The Bishops believed that although it was registered by Oblates, the land belonged to the Church rather than to the Congregation. Since both the Oblates and the Oregon Church were in financial need, neither would give up what they considered to be their due right.

A second area of grievance arose when Rome made ecclesiastical changes in Oregon whereby some of the Oblate missions were placed under the jurisdiction of Archbishop Blanchet and some, including Oblate headquarters at Olympia, were placed under the direction of Magloire Blanchet. Magloire Blanchet and the Oblates had clashed as early as 1847 when the newly-arrived French missionaries met the French-Canadian Bishop and three secular priests at St. Louis, Missouri, en route to Oregon. Blanchet understood that the Oblates would not be arriving for several months and, as he had made no travel arrangements for them, he was not entirely pleased to see them. When they came under his jurisdiction, the Bishop decided to confine his Oblates to their work among the Indians, and, enforcing this policy, he removed them from Olympia where they were ministering to white settlers, and put a diocesan priest in charge.[15] This removed a much needed source of income from the Oblates. This "in-fighting" was not conducive to productive work, but a greater difficulty was provided by the Indians themselves.

Of all the difficulties encountered by the Oblates in their years in Oregon, none was more universal than the nomadic lifestyle of the Indians and the detrimental effects of Indian-white contact. The method of rectifying these problems was also universal. Throughout North America — as in South America, Africa and Asia — missionaries of all denominations encouraged the indigenous people, regardless of their cultural development, to settle in one area and to follow agricultural pursuits. To alleviate problems caused by native-white contact, efforts were made to isolate the aborigines as far as possible. The missionaries of the Pacific Northwest were no exception.[16]

The Oregon Oblate who gave the most thought to the problems and frustrations of working as circuit missionaries among nomadic Indians was Paul Durieu. He noted that regardless of the responsiveness of groups of Indians, follow-up work was necessarily spasmodic because of the size of the territory to be covered and the scarcity of priests. The most successful Oblate work was done at Olympia where groups from various tribes stayed two or three weeks. During this time they learnt the catechism, prayers, and hymns. Copies of the Catholic Ladder were distributed to willing Indian catechists as per Blanchet's instructions. Baptism, however, was restricted to infants and elderly Indians in danger of death, and to those who had rejected Indian ways for a full year. Without constant attention and guidance, few Indians kept their promises to give up superstitions, polygamy, gambling, and liquor. Durieu gave a great deal of thought to these difficulties and gradually formed a practical solution to them.[17]

Durieu took the first elements of his method of Catholicization from the "Instructions on Foreign Missions" which de Mazenod had added to the *Constitution and Rules* in 1853. In part the founder wrote:

> . . . far from thinking it incongruent with their ministry to train the Indians to the duties of civil life, the Oblates will consider it as intimately connected with the mission's welfare and as most fit to the obtaining of better results. Every means should therefore be taken to bring the nomad tribes to abandon their wandering life and to build houses, cultivate fields and practise the elementary crafts of civilized life.

De Mazenod specified that the missionaries should keep traditionally warring tribes peaceful and promote interior tribal harmony, industry, and labour. Although he stated clearly that the Oblates should "never take upon themselves the government of the tribes," nevertheless, when tribal elections were held they were to procure votes for those capable of fulfilling the office, "namely of governing according to the dictates of Religion and Justice."[18] This mandate gave Durieu the freedom to contemplate the establishment of Christian Indian communities.

"Durieu's System" (as it became known) saw the creation of a Catholic Indian state in every willing Indian village. An administration was created under the direct authority of the Bishop, with local missionaries acting as the initial supervisors. The administration consisted of: the Chief and a sub-Chief, who were responsible for keeping undesirable white men (e.g., bootleggers) away from their people; one or two watchmen who ensured that both adults and children attended religious instruction and did not return to now-forbidden Indian practises; policemen who carried out punishments — the collecting of fines or, occasionally, physical punishment for frequent repeaters — passed down by the Chief on those who lapsed into the old ways (although drunkenness was one of the gravest transgressions); catechists who were responsible for teaching religious knowledge to both adults and children and "la cloche" men, bell-ringers, sometimes known as "ting ting" men, who summoned the people to church three times daily.[19]

In accepting the new administration, the Indians had to reject forever all tribal celebrations, all patronage of the medicine man or shaman, intoxicants and gambling. Sunday observance was strictly enforced. Weekday attendance at Mass (whenever possible) or at daily prayer and catechism sessions was mandatory. Marriages had to have the priest's consent and leisure activities were frowned upon unless all necessary work was completed.[20] Every aspect of life operated under puritanical restrictions. For example, boys and girls could not play together, women and girls could never be alone (especially at night), any man or grown boy who entered the room of a woman when she was alone and engaged her in conversation had to be punished, and the Indians were forbidden to sing love songs or songs associated with gambling or medicine men. Feast days held by the Church were to be celebrated in great style, with processions and pageantry, special services, religious plays, even, on occasion, firework displays.

This detail came later, but Father Durieu worked out the System's basic structure in Oregon. In later years Durieu explained in a letter to a fellow missionary what motivated him to set up such a rigid system. "To bring the Indian to lead a Christian life" he wrote, "the missionary must exercise upon them a twofold action. A destructive action, in destroying sin wherever it flourishes and a formative action, in moulding the inner man by instruction, preaching and the reception of the sacraments." He went on to say that sin had to be destroyed by "repressing and punishing it relentlessly as an evil, horrible, and degrading thing." The missionary had to inculcate "horror, fear and flight from sin" and the repression of evil among people whom Durieu considered would easily revert to pagan ways if not attended to unceasingly, could only be accomplished through self-help.[21]

Although Durieu worked out his system for use in Oregon it was applied there only briefly. The continued violence of the Yakima War, the destruction of Oblate cabins and chapels by both Indians and volunteer Indian fighters forced all but Father Pandosy (who appears to have remained in the war zone) to retire in 1856 to Olympia. There the Oblates continued work among the Puget Sound Indians and formulated plans to abandon Oregon. Before his return to France in 1857, Superior Father Ricard urged de

Mazenod to seriously consider removing the Oblates to the new diocese of Vancouver Island and New Caledonia. Bishop Demers, who had no priests for his vast territory, had several times tried to persuade the Oblates to assist him. When in 1858, the Oblates, now under the direction of an acting-superior, Louis D'herbomez (his permanent appointment was made in 1859), finally indicated interest, Demers urged them to make an early commitment with a familiar theme: "you must go as soon as possible into the Interior of the country as it is to be feared that the Hudson's Bay Company will send to that area Protestant ministers. . . ." D'herbomez acknowledged a similar concern when he wrote to de Mazenod:

> . . . the field which opens up before us is vast and there is much to be done. The fight that lies ahead will be long and hard, as Protestant ministers are coming in ever increasing numbers. We must not let them get ahead of us.[22]

This was a theme to which D'herbomez would return time and time again.

One of D'herbomez's first actions as acting-Superior was to withdraw the Oblates from Nisqually "as the Bishop of that See wished to impose upon them conditions incompatible with the spirit of their vocation."[23] The feuding between the French and the French Canadians had not abated and in order to avoid similar problems the Oblates sought to make autonomy a condition of their taking up work in British Columbia. They believed it was essential that New Caledonia be taken from Bishop Demers' jurisdiction and placed in the hands of a religious order with the Bishop or Vicar-Apostolic in charge of the new district a member of that order. The Oblates at Olympia did not specify that their order should be chosen. They suggested simply that for the good of future work any order chosen be given autonomy. In 1858, de Mazenod sent a Canonical visitor, Father François Bermond, to investigate the situation. Like the Oregon Oblates, Bermond thought the missionaries should accept Bishop Demers' pressing request and move to British Columbia where they could hope for autonomy. To Father de Mazenod, he recommended that the Oblates should work temporarily under the authority of Bishop Demers, although it would be better if eventually the territory were confined exclusively to them as a new Vicariate Apostolic.[24] Acting on this report, the Oblate Council in France requested Rome to establish an autonomous Vicariate for the Oblates in New Caledonia.

While negotiations with Rome continued Fathers D'herbomez and Richard with Brothers Surel and Janin moved to Esquimalt in July 1858. The Oblate withdrawal from Oregon was gradual (a mission at Tulalip remained open until 1878) as Father de Mazenod insisted that established missions should not be abandoned until those in the new territory were definitely established.[25] However, the Oblates lost little time in establishing themselves firmly on Vancouver Island. Using Esquimalt as their base, they began missions among the Saanich and Cowichan Indians, explored the West Coast, and established St. Michael's Mission at Fort Rupert among the Kwakiutl on the northern tip of the Island. When a school begun by the Bishop was faced with closure because the Clerics of St. Viator (who he had brought from Quebec) could not teach in English, the Oblates took over that work. Father de Mazenod had provided in the *Constitution and Rules* for his priests and brothers to assume the role of educators:

> When the good of souls may seem to require it, and this may more easily happen in missionary countries, the Provincial (Superior) and his Council, may build or take charge of Minor Seminaries or Colleges. And in such institutions, the members of our Society will earnestly endeavour to give the young an education that is not only Christian, but literary and Scientific as well.[26]

As Bishop Demers still had no diocesan priests to help him, the missionaries also worked in the Victoria parish among the growing white population.

Because of his ever-present concern over the Protestant thrust, Father D'herbomez pleaded with de Mazenod to allow the establishment of missions on the Mainland. "Time is pressing" he urged, "the English Church have already an Episcopal See; their ministers are travelling in all directions and they know as well as we do how to choose the best places for the success of their purpose."[27] To a man who had come to envision British Columbia as a "second California" where the Church would flourish among the increasing numbers of French, Irish, Canadian, Italian, Spanish and Mexican immigrants,[28] the spread of Protestant faiths was a very real threat.

In March 1859, Father D'herbomez closed down the missions in the Yakima territory and sent Father Pandosy to open a mission for both Indians and whites in the Okanagan Valley. This he hoped would be partly supported by contributions from the numerous miners trekking to the newly discovered gold-fields of British Columbia. The arrival from France of two new priests, Father Leon

Fouquet and Father Charles Grandidier, and the closure of St. Joseph's Olympia, allowed the Superior to open further missions on the Mainland. In 1860, the Oblates founded St. Charles, New Westminster, and mission outposts at Fort Douglas, Yale, and Hope; in 1861 they established St. Mary's on the Fraser River at the present site of Mission City.

During the time of these advances the Oblates remained under the direction of Bishop Demers, a situation that was far from satisfactory. As the Oblates were now so well-established in many areas other than Indian mission work, Rome considered making an Oblate co-adjuter with Bishop Demers. This did not please the Bishop who wished a French-Canadian assistant. The Oblate takeover of so many projects appears to have angered Demers who, like the Blanchets, preferred to see the French missionaries involved only in Indian work. A political struggle with both the Bishop and the Oblates petitioning Rome ensued. In a letter to Rome, de Mazenod's successor Father Fabre (de Mazenod died in May 1861) wrote that the establishment of the Vicariate should be given priority so that the Oblates could be "supported and encouraged in their efforts instead of having obstacles continually put in their way."[29] While the struggle for a satisfactory administrative situation continued, Oblate missionaries in British Columbia began the task of drawing the native peoples to Catholicism.

Away from the dominance of the Blanchets, the Oblates could now consider their own method of christianization. As there was still a shortage of priests and lay Brothers, and an even greater territory to cover, the use of the Catholic Ladder and Indian catechists was not abandoned entirely. But when mission sites were selected, sufficient land was purchased to enable the missionaries to establish Christian Indians in the vicinity of the mission. At every mission centre the Oblates made an effort to persuade the Indians to accept Father Durieu's plan and begin the formation of Catholic Indian communities.

In 1864, Rome granted the autonomy the Oblates desired. Father D'herbomez, given the honorary title Bishop of the Melitopolis, combined the roles of Director of Oblate Missions in the Northwest and ecclesiastical leader of the Mainland Vicariate of British Columbia. He was now in a position to use his priests and brothers as he so desired. The new situation, however, placed Bishop D'herbomez in the role of ecclesiastical leader. Together with the development of Indian missions, he had to create an adequate financial base to build churches, residences, schools, and charitable institutions. Autonomy also forced each Oblate into a dual role. The missionaries were the Vicariate's only priests and, as such, they were now responsible for all the whites as well as the Indians of Mainland British Columbia. Conflict between denominations still pressured the various churches and, worried by the publication of a letter of the Anglican Bishop of Victoria, Bishop Hill, urging bishops, ministers, teachers, and catechists from England "to prevent the expansion of the Catholic Church in British Columbia,"[30] D'herbomez impressed upon Father Fabre the urgent need for more missionaries. He particularly requested English-speaking ones who could set up Catholic schools.

By 1864, the failures in Oregon were long passed; yet their influence remained in force. Difficulties presented by inter-denominational competition was long to influence a bishop charged with directing the growth and development of the Ecclesiastical Church in British Columbia. Conflict with French-Canadian church leaders had resulted in autonomy, but was also to result in the deployment of few men and resources over a vast territory. The nomadic lifestyle of the Indians which severely limited conversion led to the creation of the Durieu System, an organization which found favour with many Indian bands in British Columbia, but which would one day become a controversial issue. With years of experience behind them, their priorities firmly established, in 1866, the Oblates decided to open a mission dedicated to St. Joseph in the Cariboo area of British Columbia; its primary purpose the conversion and spiritual guidance of the numerous Indian bands scattered throughout the area.

NOTES TO CHAPTER I

1 Correspondence of de Mazenod, Donat Lavasseur, *History of the Oblate Congregation*, Ottawa, 1959, p. 50.

2 F. Lardon, O.M.I. "O.M.I. on the Pacific Coast," Manuscript, O.A., Vancouver.

3 Lavasseur, *History of the Oblate Congregation*, p. 26.

4 *Ibid.*, p. 21.

5 *Ibid.*, p. 80.

6 *The Constitutions and Rules of the Congregation of the Missionary Oblates of the Most Holy and Immaculate Virgin Mary*, Rome, 1945 edition, p. 21. (Cited hereafter as *Constitutions and Rules.*)

7 Instructions of Bishop Signay to Blanchet and Demers, April 17, 1838, Register M. Fol. 96v-99r, p. 1, A.A.Q.

[8] *Ibid.*, pp. 1-2.

[9] Francis Norbert Blanchet, *Historical Sketches of the Catholic Church in Oregon 1838-1878*, Washington, 1910, p. 24. (Cited hereafter as *Historical Sketches.*)

[10] *Ibid.*, p. 31.

[11] Philip Hanley, "The Catholic Ladder and Missionary Activity in the Pacific Northwest," Rome, 1965, p. 5.

[12] Blanchet, *Historical Sketches,* p. 50.

[13] Lardon, "O.M.I. on the Pacific Coast," p. 10.

[14] *Ibid.*, p. 29.

[15] *Ibid.*, p. 37.

[16] William Duncan of Metlakatla is the best known of such missionaries; others emulated his method but without such spectacular success.

[17] P. Besson, *Un Missionaire d'Autrefois: Paul Durieu O.M.I.*, Marseilles, 1962, p. 215.

[18] "Instructions of Our Venerated Father," insert in *Constitutions and Rules,* Rome, 1936 edition, p. 13. A.D.

[19] Information from Besson, *Un Missionaire d'Autrefois*; Edwin M. Lemert, "The Life and Death of an Indian State," *Human Organization* (Vol. 13, No. 3, 1954); Bishop E. N. Bunoz, "Catholic Action and the Durieu System, 1941," Oblate History, Microfilm, U.B.C. (Cited hereafter as Oblate History, U.B.C.)

[20] According to Bishop Bunoz, who accompanied Bishop Durieu on visits to Sechelt, Durieu once removed a football from the Indian boys because they had neglected work.

[21] Bishop Durieu to Father LeJacq, November 27, 1883, Durieu Correspondence, A.D.

[22] Lardon, "O.M.I. on the Pacific Coast," pp. 21-26.

[23] Adrian Morice, *History of the Catholic Church in Western Canada,* Vol. 1, Toronto, 1910, p. 219.

[24] Correspondence of Father Casimir Aubert Lardon, "O.M.I. on the Pacific Coast," p. 44.

[25] *Ibid.*, p. 46.

[26] "The Direction of Youth," *Constitution and Rules,* 1945, p. 46.

[27] Bishop D'herbomez to de Mazenod, April 6, 1859, D'herbomez Correspondence. A.D. Ottawa.

[28] Report of the Vicariate of British Columbia, 1861, File No. PB517, A.D.

[29] Father Fabre (new Superior General) to Cardinal Barnabo in Rome, February 14, 1862, Lardon, "O.M.I. on the Pacific Coast," p. 77.

[30] Lardon, "O.M.I. on the Pacific Coast," p. 68.

Shuswap Shaman performing healing ceremony in subterranean winter dwelling.

Chapter II

THE PEOPLE AND RELIGION

The Indians who came under the spiritual guardianship of St. Joseph's Mission were of two ethnic groups, Athapascan and Interior Salish. The Athapascans were the Chilcotin who lived primarily in the valley of the Chilcotin river, west of the Mission, the Lower Carrier to the northwest and immediate north of St. Joseph's, and Upper Carriers and Babines who lived in the far north and northeast of the Mission, and for whom in 1871, the Oblates opened a separate mission, Our Lady of Good Hope, Stuart Lake. The Interior Salish were the Shuswap who lived in the immediate vicinity of St. Joseph's and to the south and southeast as far as Clinton and Canim Lake respectively. Prior to the appearance of the white men, these diverse peoples had shared a common hunting and fishing economy but the Chilcotin and the Shuswap were bitter enemies while the Chilcotin and Carrier were trading partners. The response of the Cariboo Indians to the invasion of their territory by fur-traders, miners, and settlers had been far from uniform.

The Cariboo Indians first entered white British Columbia history in the summer of 1793 when Alexander McKenzie passed through their territory on his journey to the Pacific. McKenzie wrote in his journal of meeting Carrier and Shuswap Indians. In 1805, Simon Fraser crossed the Rocky Mountains into northern British Columbia and established the first fur-trading post among the Carriers at McLeod Lake. The following year he built Fort St. James at the south end of Stuart Lake and a post on Fraser Lake; in 1807, Fraser erected Fort George at the confluence of the Fraser and Nechako rivers. All these Forts were in the Carrier country north of the Cariboo. In 1806, passing through the Cariboo during the course of his famous journey to the Pacific, Fraser wrote of meeting a tribe who called themselves "Chilk-odins"; these were the fiercely independent Chilcotins, the Cariboo's third Indian group.

For fifteen years Indians from the Cariboo region travelled to Fort George to trade their furs. It was not until the Northwest Company amalgamated with the Hudson's Bay Company in 1821 that the first trading post was erected in the Cariboo. Until 1821, the northern trading posts had received their supplies and trade goods from Montreal. This necessitated long journeys across the plains and the mountains. To avoid the large expense involved in this process, the Hudson's Bay Company decided to send supplies from Fort Vancouver in Oregon via the Columbia River and the Okanagan Valley, to the newly erected Fort Thompson (Kamloops) and finally to a new depot established on the Fraser River at Alexandria.[1]

Fort Alexandria became "the paradise of New Caledonia" for the fur traders, and the primary source of white contact for the Cariboo's Indians. It was situated in comparatively open country enabling the fort personnel to grow a fair quantity of wheat in addition to many vegetables. To take advantage of this fortunate situation and to lessen dependency on the delivery of flour from Fort Vancouver, Chief Factor Peter Skene Ogden built at Alexandria the first flour mill in British Columbia.[2] Unlike the northern posts where boredom was often the norm, Fort Alexandria was a centre of high activity. Numerous Carrier Indians lived in the vicinity and they, together with Shuswap from the south, were the most frequent visitors, coming either to trade their furs or obtain credit for goods at the store. The Company employees were fairly well occupied grinding flour, attending to the vegetable gardens, building and repairing numerous salmon fishing weirs, cutting hay, hunting game, and maintaining the fort buildings. Once a year the pack train arrived from Fort Vancouver, the horses laden with goods and supplies for the northern posts. This cargo was transferred to pack trains which then headed north. Furs collected at the Fort were sent south. Unless he had a penchant for idleness, an employee at Fort Alexandria could consider himself fortunate to be posted where there was little chance of boredom, a variety of foods, and where fish and game were plentiful; one sent to the second fort established in the Cariboo might, with little exaggeration, consider himself condemned to a miserable, fearful existence.

Few Chilcotin Indians appeared at Fort Alexandria with furs to trade; yet the Chilcotin territory was not poor in furs. Animosity between the Chilcotin and Indians living at the Fort was partly responsible and a blood feud between the two groups delayed the establishment of a post on the Chilcotin river.[3] Fort Chilcotin was eventually built in 1829 but had to be abandoned a year later because of Indian threats of violence against the personnel. The Indians then burnt it to the ground. A second attempt was made to induce the Chilcotin to become trappers for the company. Two forts were built, one to replace Fort Chilcotin and a second at Kluskus, on the northern border of Chilcotin territory. Neither was a success, and the employees lived under strained circumstances.[4] The Chilcotin had adequate commerce with the coastal Indians, and the Kluskus Fort stood between them and their trading partners. They considered the white company as a rival and they could see little or no advantage in commercial intercourse.[5] In 1837, a feud broke out between the Chilcotin and Baptiste Lapierre, a company employee at Fort Chilcotin and Lapierre's co-workers feared for their lives. Fort Chilcotin was finally abandoned in 1844. The depot at Kluskus remained in operation only a little longer.[6]

When the gold rush of 1858 brought miners and settlers to the Cariboo, Indian response was equally polarized. Some Indians, predominantly Shuswap, took advantage of the employment opportunities opened up by the operation of mines, farms, and ranches. The Chilcotin, angered by the intrusion of whites, attacked and killed members of a surveying party and a miner camping at a Chilcotin campsite in British Columbia's only Indian massacre. Gregarious and friendly for the most part (although there were some attacks on miners), the Shuswap and Carrier accepted the white man, taking advantage of what he had to offer, apparently without too much visible animosity; an aloof and feared people — even in later years ranchers in the Chilcotin area had to rope and brand their herds before entering Chilcotin territory because the Shuswap they hired refused, through fear, to enter the district[7] — the Chilcotin openly opposed the newcomers.

Fortunately for the Oblates opening St. Joseph's Mission most of the Indians of Cariboo, for a variety of reasons, were pre-disposed to welcome missionaries. Prior to the arrival of white men, all these Indians held their own religious beliefs. With the exception of the Chilcotin, aspects of Indian religion synchronized with Christianity and this synchronization made at least some Catholic truths comprehensible to the Indians.

The Shuswap believed in two great spirits they called the Old-One and Coyote.[8] The Old-One, chief of the ancient world, was all-powerful. He regulated the seasons, weather and animals — the last he commanded to multiply. He led different tribes into the country which they now inherit and gave them the languages they were to speak. When the Old-One had finished his work, he disappeared towards the east; some say he went to the sky where he watched the earth. Some believed he lived in a spirit land from which he sometimes sent messengers. The Indians expected him to return some day and make the world a better place.

The Old-One had as his chief assistant, or transformer, a spirit called Coyote. Although the description of Coyote varies somewhat from the Christian idea of Jesus — Coyote was sometimes vain, lazy and mischievous — there were enough similarities between the two figures to ensure familiarity for the Indians. Coyote was sent by the Old-One to travel over the world and put it to rights. He was gifted with powers beyond those of other spirits and had great knowledge. It was said that he would either precede or accompany the Old-One on the day both returned to earth bringing with them the souls of the spirit land. This return would mark the beginning of a golden age when the dead would be re-united with the living, and everyone would live a life of ease and happiness.

It is easy to see how closely these beliefs resembled the Christian belief in God, His Son, Creation, and the Apocalypse. Of even greater importance to the missionaries was the Shuswap belief that the apocalyptic event would be preceded by the appearance on earth of one or more messengers from the Old-One who were to make the world a place of happiness for both the living and the dead. When the Indians first met Catholic priests, they are said to have believed them to be these messengers.

Other similarities aided synchronization. The Shuswap believed in souls and guardian-spirits and held two great festivals a year, at mid-summer and mid-winter. They believed that on leaving the body, souls travelled to a far place "somewhere beyond or at the edge of the world," a spirit land where it was always warm, where berries were always ripe, grass always greener, flowers profuse, and flies and mosquitoes were non-existant. Christian belief in immortality of the soul and the concept of heaven would have been perfectly comprehensible to the Shuswap.

Like the Shuswap, the Catholic religion accepted and proclaimed the existence of guardian spirits; each person was said to have a guardian angel whose role was to protect its charge from evil. Although the Shuswap guardian spirits protected the Indians from physical harm — women did not pass the back or the head of a man lying down without warning him because they might startle the man and his guardian spirit might harm the women — and took the form of animals, birds, and other natural elements, in this Catholic belief the Indians would have recognized a similarity to their own.

The most notable festivals held by the Shuswap were the mid-summer and mid-winter ghost or circle dance celebrations. On the morning of the dance they fasted and washed; at noon they feasted and prayed to the Chief of the Dead to preserve them from all harm. At the coming of the missionaries several bands of Shuswap elevated this god to the rank of a sky deity and identified him with the Christian God. In view of the timings of these festivals and the special preparations, particularly fasting, which accompanied them, the Indians were able to relate more easily to the Christian feasts of Christmas and Easter.

Shuswap pre-white contact religion lent itself to synchronization with Catholicism; the Carrier pre-contact religion had a similar nature. The natural religious beliefs of the Carriers — which were said to be "a blend of beliefs current among neighbouring tribes"[9] — contained five elements of basic Catholic belief: belief in a supreme spirit, group worship, belief in a soul and a soul's after-life, belief in personal spirits and belief in confession to a medicine man in times of sickness or approaching death. Although the first three beliefs are said to have been lightly held,[10] they nevertheless gave some familiarity to missionary talk of God, the necessity for church attendance, and the importance of the soul. Since the Carriers offered food and drink to their sky god when asking for favours, the priests' action of offering bread and wine at the Mass would be understandable. And Carrier belief in an after-life for the soul which was in a shadowy world or in some far away land in the west strongly resembled the Christian notion of the soul leaving the body at death.

The strongest Carrier belief was their belief in spirits, the servants of a supreme being, whose objectives were to protect or harm the individual. As with the Shuswap, the Catholic concept of angels' and devils' roles in society was not new to the Carriers. A second purely Catholic concept observed by a fur-company clerk who lived among the Carrier peoples from 1810-1819 was that of confession. Danial Harmon wrote:

When the Carriers are severely sick, they often think that they shall not recover unless they divulge to a priest or a magician every crime which they may have committed, which has hitherto been kept a secret.[11]

Although motives were often different, outward manifestations of religious beliefs were close enough to allow both the Shuswap and Carrier Indians to experience the similarities between their natural religion and that of the missionaries. By the mid-nineteenth century, many Catholic elements had been incorporated into the Carrier (and their neighbour's, the Sekani) religion through the "prophet movement."

The "prophet movement" manifested itself in British Columbia in the early decades of the nineteenth century.[12] Initially, it involved Indians who had travelled long distances from their country and had come into contact with various missionary groups. On their return to their people, these "native prophets" acted the role of the missionaries, imitating aspects of Christian ritual. The northern Carriers had their own prophet, Beni, who having temporarily disappeared from his tribe (and possibly coming in contact with Russian missionaries in Alaska) returned and taught his people to say prayers, make the sign of the cross, repent, and lead a new life. His ideas were supposed to have come through visions, and he attracted a large following.

About 1834, a movement that affected a larger area spread rapidly through the southern Carriers. In 1829, two Indians, one a Spokane, the other a Kutenai, returned to their homes after being baptized and educated by Oblate missionaries in the Red River (Manitoba) area. One of the Indians, Spokane Gerry, preached his new religion among his people and his newly acquired beliefs were passed from tribe to tribe, travelling great distances.[13] John McLean, a trader at Fort St. James, wrote of the movement reaching his area "where it spread with amazing rapidity all over the country."[14] Singing and dancing, use of Catholic rituals and gestures were incorporated into Carrier religious festivities. "Prophet dances" included the observance of a Sabbath, the use of written language for preaching, the sign of the cross, and terms such as "Jesus Christ" and "Amen." This indirect contact with Christianity was reinforced by two forms of direct contact. One was via the personnel of the fur-trade, the other via the brief but important visitations of Catholic priests.

With one or two exceptions, fur-trade personnel did not attempt to bring Christianity to the Indians. On the contrary, according to Father Morice who recorded much of the history of these early contacts,

> . . . Instead of lifting the lower race up to the standard of Christianized Europeans, the fur-trade personnel in too many cases, stooped to the level of the savages they had come to as the representatives of a wonderful civilization. Gambling, Indian-fashion dancing, face-painting, potlatching or heathen feasting, rendering murder for murder, the lax observation of the Lord's Day, disregard of the sanctity of marriage ties . . . were not only countenanced, but actually practised by the company's officers and servants.[15]

It would appear from Father Morice's statement that the Indians saw little evidence of white-Christian religious beliefs. There were however exceptions. French-Canadian trappers and Roman Catholic Iroquois from eastern Canada employed by the fur companies had to some extent familiarized the Carriers and Shuswap with Catholic ways. While it is not logical to suppose that these men were openly devout practising Catholics while away from their homes in the East, there was a time when even the most Indianized fur-trade men would return to their religion. This would be at the birth of their children. A child of "country marriages" between a French Canadian and an Indian woman would undoubtedly have been baptized. Believing as all Catholics did that an unbaptized child could not enter heaven, and given the mortality rate among young children, the Catholic partner would himself administer the act of baptism until such time as a priest was available to solemnize it. In this way, the French Canadians familiarized the Indians with the act of admission to the Church.

According to famed ethnologist Diamond Jenness, the Iroquois in the service of the trading companies implanted the idea of monotheism among the northern Carrier.[16] Certainly there were many Iroquois in the Cariboo. They had a permanent village at Tête Jaune Cache which is said to have been named for "a yellow-haired Iroquois trapper." These trappers and hunters occasionally abducted and married Shuswap girls[17] thereby providing another, if somewhat reluctant, avenue for the communication of Catholicism.

Although discouraged by company policy from influencing Indian social structure — at least in any way that might be harmful to fur-trade relationships — some fur-trade personnel made positive attempts to convert the Indians who came to trade. William Mc-

Bean, a company clerk, became famous among the Carrier "as a sort of lay preacher whose hybrid religion betrayed his own Cree origin, since it consisted mostly of vague notions about the Deity and the primary percepts of the natural law." McBean's religious observances were similar to those of the "prophets" and were "reduced to shouting and dancing."[18] Because of his resemblance to the prophets, Indian response to McBean was probably at least indulgent and curious. A second company clerk who received little response from the Carriers to his attempts at proslytization was Daniel Harmon. Harmon felt it was his duty to instruct the Indians whenever the opportunity arose:

> I have often told them it is that Being alone who made the Sun, Moon, Stars and this world and everything that is in it, who has power or influence over the wind and weather as well as of the lives of these creatures too, and yet none of them appear to believe me.

Harmon's phlegmatic approach apparently lacked appeal, yet he continued to pursue the subject of white Christianity as often as he could.[19]

The one group of Cariboo Indians who remained aloof from any Christian influence was the Chilcotin. To begin with, the Chilcotin natural religious beliefs were non-compatible with Christianity. While they believed in guardian spirits, the Chilcotin did not believe in life after death or the "happy hunting ground" concept. On the contrary, they are said to have had an active skepticism regarding such ideas.[20] Because of their aversion to the white fur-trade, Chilcotin contact with fur-trade personnel was minimal and, since the traders unlucky enough to be sent to the short-lived Fort Chilcotin were in constant fear of their lives, it is unlikely that any communication of Christian theology took place. It was not until the first visits of Catholic priests in the 1940's that the Chilcotin encountered Christianity.

Direct knowledge of Catholic missionaries began in 1841 when Modeste Demers left Oregon and travelled north to seek out the Indians of New Caledonia and judge their receptivity of Catholicism. Baptizing children whenever possible, Demers reached the Williams Lake area of Cariboo via Fort Okanagan and Fort Thompson (Kamloops). He preached to a local Shuswap band led by Chief William whom he requested to build a small church. Promising to visit them on his return journey, Demers travelled on to Fort Alexandria, where he preached to the Indians visiting the

Fort, mostly Carrier. After baptizing twenty-eight children (many the children of French Canadians and Indian women), he left for a three-day visit to Stuart Lake. Demers then returned to Fort Alexandria where he spent the winter months preaching daily to the Indians who, at his request, began construction of a chapel. In the spring, leaving copies of the Catholic Ladder with the Chiefs,[21] Demers returned to the Williams Lake area where he preached to the Indians of Chimney Creek, Alkali Lake, and Soda Creek. At Chimney Creek, on the property now referred to as the "Milk Ranch," Chief William's band had erected a small church and a house for the priest. Before returning to Oregon, Demers taught the Shuswap short prayers and hymns which the Indians, in turn, taught their children. Many years later one of these children, Captain Charlie of Soda Creek, sang the hymns he had learnt from his parents for an Oblate missionary. At Chimney Creek a large cross was built to commemorate the Demers' visit and when this Indian band moved to Williams Lake about 1863, they took the cross with them.[22]

In June 1845, a Jesuit missionary Father John Nobili travelled with the fur brigade from Oregon to the Cariboo where he remained until 1847. Unlike Demers he encountered not only Shuswap and Carriers but also the "terrible Chilcotin." An incident recorded in 1873 by a Protestant minister, Reverend R. C. Lundin-Brown, reveals how even the skeptical Chilcotin displayed a keen interest in Christianity by the tenacity with which they clung to Father Nobili's teachings.

While on a visit to Fort Simpson in 1861, Lundin-Brown took the opportunity to preach to a gathering of Indians who were in the area.[23] A group of Chilcotin, among them Klatsassan the warrior chief who was to become notorious for his leadership of the Waddington Massacre, listened to the minister's preaching, then approached him. Klatsassan began to search the startled man who asked what the Indian wanted. Klatsassan "pulled out of his bosum a crucifix which was tied around his neck." He wanted to see the minister's crucifix for "he had been taught to recognize it as the mark of the true priest." Reverend Brown wrote in his memoirs:

I was not the first to preach Christianity to his tribe. Some twenty years previously, certain Roman Catholic missionaries had crossed over from Canada into British Columbia and with their wonted zeal had preached to the natives. Probably from want of time they did not teach them very much of religion, but what they did teach had been received with ardour and retained with amazing fidelity.

Since Father Nobili had remained in Chilcotin country for only twelve days, and Demers had not visited them at all, the Chilcotin had retained an interest in Christianity based on a brief visit almost twenty years previously. This Chilcotin interest in something related to white society in those early contact years appears to be out of character, but in view of its assertion by an Anglican minister in the days when it was more popular for one denomination to malign the work of another than to signal its success, Chilcotin response cannot be doubted.

In addition to these favourable conditions, two other circumstances favoured the success of St. Joseph's. Along with missionaries of other denominations, the Oblates realized that the moral and social concepts that they taught their prospective converts could not readily be seen in frontier society. It was advisable therefore, that the Indians, who ironically were expected to be more Christian than the Christian society they had come in contact with, should be separated from any aspect of civilization other than the Churches.[24] In an area such as the Cariboo, this was at least feasible. Although the establishment of the fur-trade posts had provided some of the usual social and economic contact problems, the effects were not on the scale encountered near the fast developing areas of the Lower Mainland. In the case of the Chilcotin of course the effects were minimal.

From 1858, waves of gold-seekers provided instant pockets of white population, making drink and opportunities for prostitution available particularly to those Indians who had camps in the mining area. In 1866, an Oblate missionary wrote of Shuswap Indian girls in the mining area who had become prostitutes.[25] Those Indians who worked alongside whites were sure to be influenced also, in some respects. In general, however, large numbers of Cariboo's three tribes remained isolated from white communities. Bishop D'herbomez was aware from his own experience of the advantage to conversion in this isolation. And he had been reminded of it by Demers who, urging the opening of a Mission in the interior eight years earlier, asserted that more good could be done among the interior tribes than among those of the Lower Fraser who had been "greatly affected by the bad example of worthless white people."[26] By the time D'herbomez was able to comply with Demers' wishes, contact with white population had intensified in Cariboo but, compared with other areas of missionary endeavour, it had not proved too damaging.

Equally favourable to the success of St. Joseph's was the absence of concerted denominational competition for the allegiance of the Indians. In 1866, the Cariboo was still in effect "unclaimed" missionary territory. In British Columbia, doubtless because of their bad experience in Oregon, the Oblates did not establish missions in direct competition with Protestant ones. Although Anglicans and other Protestant ministers had settled in Cariboo ahead of the Oblates, by 1866, in response to a decline in gold-seeking activities, they had left. Public spiritual activity was reduced to religious meetings regularly held in Cambrian Hall, Barkerville, where English and Welsh services were held every alternate Sunday.[27] There was no ordained minister, and no attempts appear to have been made by any denomination to establish missionary work among the Indians. Initially, the Oblates had the field entirely to themselves. Under these propitious circumstances, St. Joseph's missionaries began their work.

NOTES TO CHAPTER II

1 Margaret Ormsby, *British Columbia: A History*, Vancouver, 1958, p. 71.

2 *Ibid.*

3 Adrian Morice, *The History of the Northern Interior of British Columbia*, new edition, Smithers, 1978, p. 124. (Cited hereafter as *The History of the Northern Interior.*)

4 Morice, *The History of the Northern Interior*, pp. 181-184.

5 E. S. Hewlett, "The Chilcotin Uprising of 1854," *B.C. Studies*, No. 19 (August 1973), p. 52.

6 Morice, *The History of the Northern Interior*, p. 123.

7 George Terry, "History and Legends of the Chilcotin," Williams Lake, 1958, p. 14. P.H.B.C.

8 Material of Shuswap religion is taken from James Teit, "The Shuswap," *Memoir of the American Museum of Natural History*, Vol. 11 (Part 7), 1909.

9 Diamond Jenness, *The Indians of Canada*, Ottawa, 1963, p. 367.

10 *Ibid.*

11 Danial Harmon, *Sixteen Years in Indian Country, 1800-1816*, Toronto, 1957, p. 251.

12 A detailed study of the prophet movement can be found in H. E. Rumley, "Reactions to Contact and Colonization of Religious and Social Change Among the Indians of British Columbia," M.A. Thesis, U.B.C., 1973.

[13] Robin Fisher, *Contact and Conflict*, Vancouver, 1977, p. 123.

[14] Morice, *History of the Northern Interior*, p. 225.

[15] *Ibid.*, p. 115.

[16] Diamond Jenness, *The Sekani Indians of British Columbia*, Ottawa, 1937, p. 64.

[17] Teit, "The Shuswap," p. 468.

[18] Morice, *History of the Northern Interior*, p. 225.

[19] Harmon, *Sixteen in Indian Country*, p. 251.

[20] R. B. Lane, *The Cultural Relations of the Chilcotin Indians of West Central British Columbia*, Michigan, 1953, p. 57.

[21] Wilfred P. Schoenburg, *Chronicle of the Catholic History of the Pacific Northwest, 1743-1960*, Portland, 1962, p. 12.

[22] Father François Marie Thomas, "Memoirs," Manuscript, O.A. Vancouver.

[23] Information taken from R. C. Lundin-Brown, *Klatsassen and Other Reminiscenses of Missionary Life in British Columbia*, London, 1873.

[24] Robert Berkhofer Jr., "Model Zions for the American Indian," *American Quarterly*, Vol. 15, 1963, p. 187.

[25] Father James Maria McGuckin to Bishop Louis D'herbomez, November 1, 1866, Oblate History, U.B.C.

[26] Bishop Modeste Demers to D'herbomez, March 13, 1858, Oblate History, U.B.C.

[27] *Cariboo Sentinal*, June 11, 1868.

Father Jayol teaching the first group of Indians at the Mission in 1867.

Chapter III

"THE BRIGHTEST HOPES"

On Saturday, August 18, 1866, Father James Maria McGuckin O.M.I. alighted from the New Westminster stagecoach in Richfield, at that time the most prosperous of three mining communities centred around gold claims on Williams Creek in the Cariboo. Richfield was established in 1862. At first named the town of Williams Creek, it was later changed to Richfield by Lieutenant Palmer, Deputy Commissioner of Lands and Works. In July 1863, with Judge Matthew Baillie-Begbie officiating, a second town, Cameronton, was established around the gold claim of one Mr. Cameron, a successful miner; this was approximately one and a half miles from Richfield. Lower Richfield, or Barkerville (to give it its later more famous name) was established also that same summer. By 1866, it was generally believed by the local population that Richfield was destined to become the most important of the three. Unaware that the gold which gave it life would soon peter out, and that its boom years had passed, Richfield, with its government buildings, law offices, five banks, library, churches of several Protestant denominations, fine hotels, numerous restaurants, billiard halls, a variety of stores, and more than its share of saloons, had an air of prosperity and permanency.[1]

After taking accommodation in the opulent sounding "Paris and London Hotel," owned by two Frenchmen, Father McGuckin took a walk through Richfield, and the neighbouring towns looking for a place he could use as a temporary church.[2] Patrick Kerwin, an Irish storekeeper, offered the use of his store and with willing help from friends put the place in order. A Frenchman, Monsieur Lallier, offered to prepare a room for the priest in his house. Father McGuckin accepted the use of the store but, preferring a measure of independence, on Monday morning he went looking for a cabin for himself. Unable to find one close to his temporary church "owing to the large importation of Chinamen" on the Creek, Father McGuckin finally accepted the loan of a cabin from Kerwin. The cabin was makeshift and without a stove for either heat or cooking, but it was adequate for Father McGuckin's needs. He was an Oblate missionary, and his business in Richfield was primarily concerned with the local Indian peoples. His Bishop, Louis D'herbomez, had sent him to Cariboo to select the best site for the establishment of a new mission. While in Richfield, he was to minister temporarily to the spiritual needs of the Roman Catholics living in the area and to take up collections among them both for the maintenance of the new mission and also for the support of other Church endeavours. Thus when Kerwin suggested that the priest invest one hundred dollars in a stove to make the cabin more convenient, Father McGuckin refused, explaining that he would not "spend $100 on a place of that kind, especially as very probably it would be of no use to him the next time he returned."

The missionary's attitude distressed the Irishman, and he reproached Father McGuckin:

> It is a shame to have a Priest coming here and having to look out every time for a cabin to put his head into and a house to say Mass. You must get a church and a house alongside of it to live in and not be running about this way. We have Protestant Churches and can not we build one for you? There never was a mission camp in California without a church and we must have one here also.

Despite Father McGuckin's protest that he could do nothing without the Bishop's permission, the enterprising Kerwin set out to provide the priest with "Mr. Steele's house" which was for sale at $400. The following day when the priest returned from a visit to the miners at Grouse Creek, Kerwin showed him $471 which he had collected from local miners — some of whom left money for him "sticking in the stumps of trees." Realizing that "there was no use reasoning any longer with Pat," Father McGuckin refused to be accountable for the Irishman's actions. Within a week of the missionary's arrival Kerwin had purchased Steele's house, "one of the warmest on the Creek," at the bargain price of $250. This he presented to Father McGuckin with a promise to find and pay a contractor to make any alterations necessary to turn the house into a combination church and rectory.

The priest, although embarrassed by these arrangements as he had not been instructed to acquire property in Richfield, nevertheless wrote to his Bishop urging him to authorize acceptance of the new church which Kerwin, with a touch of pride, had already named St. Patrick's — subject of course to the Bishop's approval. The missionary also requested permission to return to Richfield and spend the winter with the enthusiastic Catholic population after he had settled the situation of the new mission. In Father McGuckin's eyes such enthusiasm warranted more than passing attention by the Church.

In helping the missionary the Irish and French Catholics were not acting from purely altruistic motives. Admittedly Father McGuckin's background made him popular with the Irish. Born in Cooleystown, County Tyrone, Northern Ireland in July 1835, he had spent his youth surrounded by Orange fanaticism. At the age of fourteen he became associated with his uncle in the management of an extensive linen manufacturing business, business experience that was to prove valuable in later years. In 1860, he left Ireland to enter the novitiate of the Oblates at Sicklinghall, Yorkshire, England. His studies were completed at the Scholastic House, Marseilles, where he met Father de Mazenod, and at Inchicore near Dublin. He arrived in Victoria in 1863 and in November was ordained a priest by Bishop Demers. For three years he was vice-principal at the school taken over by the Oblates and named St. Louis' College for Boys, and, during that time, he performed parish work among the English-speaking Catholics.

Father McGuckin's correspondence reveals him to be a serious-minded young man, conscientious, practical, demanding, both of himself and others, fanatical with regard to the rules and regulations of the Order, and totally devoid of a sense of humour. Nevertheless he was an Irishman, the first and for many years the only English-speaking Oblate in British Columbia, and as such he was most welcome among the numerous Irish working the diggings in the Cariboo. But other factors influenced the Catholic population.

As Patrick Kerwin had revealed, there was a matter of pride. In July 1863,[3] a site was purchased and a contract made for the establishment of an Episcopal church in Richfield at a cost of $1200, raised by private contributions; the church was sufficiently complete by August 9th that the local minister, Reverend John Sheepshanks, assisted by the Reverend Mr. Brown of Lillooet, celebrated the first service. Two Methodist ministers, Doctor Evans and Reverend Lachler Taylor, built a meeting house in 1863 through voluntary contributions. A year later the Wesleyans and Presbyterians had chapels and a second Episcopalian church had been erected.

Cariboo's miners did not lack the comforts of religion. It was a sore point with the Catholics that Protestant churches dominated the area — although by 1865 all these churches stood empty, their ministers long departed. There was however another and more important factor behind the Catholic support.

Goldmining was a precarious business on which to build a community and from 1863, there was evidence that people were thinking in terms of more permanent enterprises. Men who had come to mine for gold had decided to settle in the Cariboo and a growing number were turning to agricultural pursuits. Some entrepreneurs turned to farming to supply gold miners with fresh vegetables, barley, pigs and chickens; some turned to dairying, supplying milk, cream, and butter. In July 1863, an early ranching pioneer named Felker had a small herd of forty cows in the meadows near Williams Creek. Settlers had come to the Cariboo, and businessmen like Kerwin who owned a store, the Frenchmen who owned a hotel, Dennis Murphy who operated a ranch and roadside inn, and Mr. Toomey who owned 150 Mile House, all saw in the establishment of a parish at Richfield a mark of permanency. The willingness with which people had contributed to the erection of the various churches indicated a strong desire for civilized development. Churches were a sign that a frontier town had taken root; that the "boom and bust" period was giving way to settlement.

Having established contact with the Catholics, Father McGuckin now turned his attention to his primary task, the choice of the new mission site. For several years prior to 1866, Bishop D'herbomez had requested the Oblates who made missionary circuits among the goldminers of Cariboo to report on any favourable site. The criteria were as follows: a convenient gathering place for the numerous Indian bands scattered throughout the 60,000 square miles of the Cariboo; close enough to a developing white community to ensure financial support from Catholics, yet isolated enough to minimize undesirable white influence; in possession of a sufficient tract of fertile land to make the mission self-supporting as soon as possible, and large enough to encompass an area on which to settle the Indians, initially when they came for instructions and celebrations, and eventually as a permanent mission-oriented group.

Fathers Leon Fouquet and Florimund Gendre (who had arrived in Victoria in 1862 with Fathers Jean Marie LeJacq and Julien Baudre) made journeys to the Cariboo in 1864 and 1865 respectively. Both concluded that either Quesnelmouth, present day

Quesnel, or Soda Creek offered good possibilities. In July 1866, Father Grandidier who had travelled to the gold fields several times, made detailed studies of possible sites.[4] Although he presented a list of eight possibilities to D'herbomez, he favoured two, a farm in the San José River Valley (named after José Tressierra, a Mexican who owned land close-by on Three Mile Creek) owned by a Mr. Pomeroy, and some unclaimed land near 141 Mile House. Dennis Murphy, who had occasionally accommodated the visiting missionaries, recommended Pomeroy's farm to the Bishop as the better buy.[5] After visiting one or two of the sites, and discussing advantages and disadvantages with Murphy, Father McGuckin decided in favour of the farm. It was as central as could be for the Indians. It stood approximately halfway between Alkali Lake and Soda Creek, an area inhabited by Shuswap Indians, and it was reasonably close to Quesnel, a regular gathering place for Carrier and, although less frequently, the Chilcotin. Only seventy miles from the mining areas of Williams Creek where Father McGuckin had received such an encouraging welcome, it was distant enough to discourage social intercourse between Indians who gathered at the Mission and the "undesirable elements" who gathered at the Creek. Most importantly, as both Fathers McGuckin and Grandidier stressed, the land had proven to be fertile, came complete with farm equipment and some stock, and could support the Mission "as soon as the first crop was in."

In April 1867, Bishop D'herbomez purchased Pomeroy's farm and this transaction marked the official beginning of St. Joseph's Mission. The purchase was delayed because Church interest in the property caused the owner to raise his original asking price. Throughout the winter months, in spite of Father McGuckin's urging, the Bishop was reluctant to pay more than $600.[6] The problem was resolved by the "diplomatic services" of Dennis Murphy and Mr. Toomey. These gentlemen bought the farm from Pomeroy for much less than he offered it to the Bishop and then sold it to Bishop D'herbomez at cost. In addition, they put in a wheat crop and Murphy gave a milk cow to the new mission. During these negotiations, mission work was begun by Father Francis Jayol, a former diocesan priest from Oregon who had joined the Oblates. Residing temporarily at Dennis Murphy's ranch at Deep Creek, he visited and preached to the local Shuswap. As soon as the sale was completed Brother Surel was sent from New Westminster to begin work on the Mission land. The choice of Brother Surel was a sound one as he was a farmer's son, and a carpenter by trade. The only habitable building on the property was a somewhat delapidated small cabin and, initially, this served Father Jayol as home, chapel and a centre to which he invited local Indians for basic instruction in the Catholic religion.

Father McGuckin urged the Bishop to consent to the replacement of the inadequate cabin by a larger house that stood on the boundary of the Mission land. Although presently tenanted by members of the Felker family, it was included in the purchase. The cabin, complained Father McGuckin, was not only in a state of disrepair but offered "no shelter for the Indians if they came in any number to be instructed." The house on the other hand was large enough to contain "a chapel, schoolroom, dormitory, kitchen, refrectory, and two or three small rooms besides." Father McGuckin wrote enthusiastically to D'herbomez that if the house was moved to a more central location on the property and some repair work done, "before the end of the summer the whole machinery of the Mission would be ready for work."

Father Jayol who was temporary mission superior remained at the Mission to deal with early adjustments, supervise the removal and renovations of the house, and to concentrate on building a strong interest in St. Joseph's among the neighbouring Shuswap. Father McGuckin had a dual role. In January 1867, he made it clear to the Bishop that the new church of St. Patrick's needed a permanent pastor:

> As William's Creek will be a great centre of the population, and there are now a good number of Catholics well disposed and desirous of attending to their religious duties . . . a Father should remain as much as possible amongst them.

In the same letter Father McGuckin announced that he had begun to teach a few boys, local Catholic children whom he instructed in their "holy religion" as well as in reading and writing. Two months later, the priest was forced to curtail this work to attend to his primary duty, contacting and preaching to the Indians.

In the spring of 1867, he visited Fort Alexandria and Quesnel where he met with members of the Carrier and Chilcotin tribes. These Indians received Father McGuckin with apparent interest and enthusiasm. During a four-day visit to Fort Alexandria, the Oblate spoke for four or five hours daily with both local Carrier and visiting Chilcotin. He reported to Bishop D'herbomez that the Alexandria Indians "desired nothing more than to know and serve God." This enthusiastic assertion was doubtless due in part to Father McGuckin's success in persuading some Carriers who were camped close to the Fort and exposed "to the worst of vices" to move back to their own people. The Chilcotin, after asking the priest to come to visit their camp, disappeared before definite plans concerning this visit could be made. Father McGuckin was the first of many Oblates to be exposed to Chilcotin inconsistency.

At Quesnel the missionary found fifty local Carriers plus a dozen or so northern Carriers from Fort George and Stuart Lake who had travelled south with the Hudson's Bay Company personnel. Again the Indians were attentive to the priest's preaching. Moreover they seemed amenable to Oblate intrusion upon their social order. When Father McGuckin explained the Durieu plan to create church officials among the bands, they responded enthusiastically. The Oblate wrote to the Bishop that "the Chief wished to elect two watchmen and two policemen whilst I was there, all the Indians desired it also, and accordingly I aided them in their choice and gave them such instruction as I judged necessary." The Chief of the Stuart Lake band, a number of whom because of their constant involvement in the fur-trade had French-Canadian blood, told the Oblate he was under instruction from his people to bring back a priest "by force, if necessary."

Notwithstanding possible Indian enthusiasm "consequent on novelty" in regard to the election of church officials for the group, this interest was an encouraging sign to the priest. The Indians were not only willing to listen to Catholic teachings, they were willing also to accept certain aspects of Durieu's plan for conversion. Indian interest might also have been aroused by Father McGuckin's concern over education for their children. He remarked to the Bishop that "all the Indians from the junction to Stuart Lake were anxious to send their children to school" and advised that the mission house be fixed up as a school for the Indians. Gratified by the Indians' positive response, Father McGuckin persuaded Bishop D'herbomez to visit the area and observe the Indians' dispositions for himself. Consequently on May 1, 1868, the Bishop arrived at St. Joseph's. With him came Father LeJacq, as new superior for the mission, and Brother Blanchet who, as one of the original five Oblates to come to Oregon, was fully conversant with the problems of new missions.

Leaving the new personnel at St. Joseph's, Bishop D'herbomez and Father McGuckin travelled north, spending five months visiting Carrier Indians. Indian response to this visit moved the Bishop to incorporate the territory of all the Northern Carriers into St. Joseph's Mission district. The Bishop also found signs of Indian enthusiasm for the new religion when, on his return journey to the Mission and on his subsequent journey back to New Westminster, he had the satisfaction of blessing ten churches and chapels: Saint Michel, Quesnel; Saint Jacques, Alexandria; Sainte Anne, Soda Creek; Saint Pierre, Alkali Lake; St. Paul, Dog Creek; Saint Gabriel, Canoe Creek; Saint Laurent, Tli-te-Naitan; Sainte Marie Refuge des Pecheurs, Pavillion; L'Assomption, Clinton, and St. Patrick's, Richfield.[7]

These early churches usually, in the case of Indian churches one-room affairs, signalled both the Church's proprietary rights and allegiance to Roman Catholicism and it was important that they be established without delay. Given the size of the territory, the small number of missionary personnel, and the time period of approximately one year, only Indian participation in the building process could have accomplished so much. Seasonal hunting and fishing trips, paid employment opportunities, and plain lack of interest in consistent work made the Indians, at best, erratic builders; but nine chapels stood as proof of their initial response to Catholicism. The tenth church to be blessed was the Richfield parish church where the congregation had purchased a bell and had had it transported from San Francisco for the occasion. The Bishop had every reason to feel optimistic as he returned to New Westminster with Father Jayol leaving further developments at St. Joseph's to Fathers LeJacq and McGuckin and Brothers Surel and Blanchet.

Bishop D'herbomez's decision to replace Father Jayol with Father LeJacq and to add Brother Blanchet to the Mission staff created a strong, versatile team at St. Joseph's. Although he was designated Superior, with the consequent administrative duties, Father LeJacq's interest lay in field work among the Indians — although his previous missionary experience had not been too encouraging. In 1863, Bishop D'herbomez had sent Fathers Pandosy and Grandidier to open a mission among the Kwakiutl Indians on Vancouver Island. When Father Grandidier became ill, Father LeJacq replaced him and spent three dismal, unsuccessful years trying to convert the resisting Indians. Those Indians who were willing to accept Christianity preferred to follow the teachings of the noted

Anglican missionary William Duncan who had previously visited the area. While with the Kwakiutl, Father LeJacq had also visited Fort Simpson and the Queen Charlotte Islands in the company of Father Fouquet but this was only a voyage of exploration, for the Bishop instructed the missionaries "not to exercise their sacred ministry to any extent amongst the Indians whom they were to visit and who had been so long under Protestant influence." Undaunted by his experience of failure on Vancouver Island — Father LeJacq later wrote of the Kwakiutl: "We taught them how to cultivate potatoes; we proved to them how stupid were their medicine men; we baptised many dying children; we brought a few to a better life and finally we left them to their fate" — the missionary gave himself wholeheartedly to the conversion of the more amenable Cariboo Indians.

He became a devoted follower of Durieu, "adhering strictly to that method of dealing with the Indians evolved by his former companion."[8] Sometimes accompanied by Brother Blanchet, he trekked happily from camp to camp under the most rigourous conditions bent on building solid Indian acceptance of the Catholic faith on the foundations laid in earlier years. Since there were twenty-two Indian bands to visit and only the winter months when the Indians settled in permanent camps ensured contact with them all, the visits often had to be brief. And because the Oblates would not baptize an Indian unless there was evidence of complete rejection of "immoral practises, pagan dances, superstitions and sorcery" for at least a year, it was imperative that the Indians accept Durieu's system as soon as possible. The appointment of a Chief, watchmen and catechists would ensure the continuity of religious ritual and teaching in the absence of the missionary. The catechism was the mainstay of this teaching and it is possible that in the early years the Oblates used the Quebec catechism that was translated into Chinook by Bishop Demers during his early years in Oregon. The Chief was expected to be a "zealous leader" of the new social order and, wherever possible, Father LeJacq and Father McGuckin encouraged the hereditary chief to accept this role. Among the Shuswaps the missionaries' task was made easier by the presence of many chiefs. The Shuswaps had war chiefs, hunting chiefs, and chiefs of dances. Some men were elected chiefs because of their wisdom, wealth, even their excellence of oratory.[9] Each band had one hereditary chief descended from the male line but if this man lacked interest in the new situation, there were obviously many others who could be approached. Both Father LeJacq and Father McGuckin implemented the system wherever the Indians were willing, but Father LeJacq, deeply committed to the Durieu method, made the greatest impact.

While personality, presentation, and Indian acceptance were important, events sometimes combined to assist Father LeJacq in his work. Father François Marie Thomas, a missionary who worked for sixty years in the Cariboo, recalled in his *Memoirs* stories of Father LeJacq that were told to him by the Indians. On one occasion Father LeJacq was called to baptize a dying Indian at Soda Creek. The harsh winter weather delayed the priest so that when he reached the camp the Indians told him the woman had died. The missionary entered her home and, sitting by the woman, said "Agathe amato" (Agatha get up). She opened her eyes, sat up, was baptized, then fell back dead. The story spread far and wide among the Indians. On another occasion, although Father LeJacq forbade him to do so, a Stikeen (Northern Carrier) brought a medicine man to cure his sick child. During an all-night dance to effect the cure, the medicine man dropped dead. Two days later the child died also. Father Thomas wrote, "this made a deep impression on all — much deeper than all Father LeJacq's sermons could make."

Although Father LeJacq travelled into Chilcotin and Carrier country, he spent time also with the Shuswap who were closer to the Mission. These Indians had the most contact with the whites and therefore in the eyes of the missionaries needed the most attention. One band in particular, a Williams Lake group, lived on mission land. Around 1870, this band was held responsible for the murder of some miners, and consequently the government would not assist them in establishing a reserve. The missionaries invited these Indians who, in legal terms, "did not own a single acre" to establish a village across the San José River from the Mission and "placed quite a large meadow at their disposal."[10] Father LeJacq spent many hours with this group, devoting every Sunday that he was not out in mission territory to their instruction. This Shuswap band came the closest to becoming a model Indian community at St. Joseph's and, along with other Shuswap bands, was a cause of great pride; as Father LeJacq wrote to his Superior General many years later:

In the beginning our Christians, especially the Shuswap part, seemed animated with the best dispositions and for several years gave their missionaries the sweetest consolation and caused them to concur the brightest hopes.[11]

A more tangible result of early missionary work was reported by Father McGuckin five years after the Mission opened. About four hundred Indians had assembled at St. Joseph's for the Easter services. They arrived on Palm Sunday and remained until Easter Monday — over a week. In accordance with Durieu's plan the Easter celebrations were very elaborate and colourful, incorporating processions, benediction and High Mass. During the eight days all baptized Indians whom the Chief, watchmen, and catechists reported as being exemplary Christians were given the second sacrament, the sacrament of Penance. Twenty adults were baptized and the same number of couples were married according to the laws of the Church.

Among the Indians were twenty Chilcotin with three of their chiefs. The appearance of the Chilcotin was most gratifying, for these people remained still the most elusive. In the winter of 1870, Father McGuckin recorded his first visit to the Chilcotin territory in a letter to Father Horris, the Vicariate Bursur: "I left St. Joseph's on the 12th November and reached Fort Alexandria in the evening of the next day. On the 15th I was told by a Chilcotin Indian that I could find a number of his countrymen camped at a distance of three days journey from Fort Alexandria, and that if I wished to visit them he would accompany me. Another Indian offered his services as interpreter. I borrowed two horses, the Chilcotin had his own horse, and on the morning of the 17th we crossed the Fraser at Fort Alexandria and started for the Chilcotin Country. The weather was very cold, the trail very bad, having on it a good deal of fallen lumber besides from 6 to 15 inches of snow all the way both going and returning. At night it froze so hard that the trees were splitting with the cold. They kept up a regular commotion all night. How comfortable you would have been there nights under a calico roof.

"On the night of the 19th at 8 or 9 p.m. wearied out with hunger and cold we reached the camp. It was snowing and blowing fearfully. The camp consisted of a few sheds made of branches. Of course we pitched once more our calico house. When we arrived all the gamblers were busy at work. But I did not mind that much so long as they did not carry into execution the oath that they pronounced 5 years ago to kill the first white man they should find in their Country. I had the usual hand shaking ceremony to go through with all except 2 men and 4 women, their wives. I baptized 18 children and one old woman. In a word, I considered my trip and mission among the terrible Chilcotin quite a success. Of all savages I have seen yet I found none so savage as the Chilcotin. They have no houses, no provisions and the majority very nearly no clothing. They number in all about *450* under four chiefs."

In spite of this apparent success, both Father LeJacq and Father McGuckin subsequently often failed to make contact with the Chilcotin even when prior arrangements had been made with various bands. In June, at the request of the three chiefs present at Easter, Father McGuckin went once more into Chilcotin country to try to capitalize on their renewed interest. He found a camp of between 250 and 300 Indians, including two groups the missionary had never seen before. These were deputations from camps of Stony Indians who lived "a semi-nomadic life" in the far west of the Chilcotin territory. According to the missionary, these Indians had "always borne a hard and bad name." In spite of their reputation, the Stonys appeared interested in what Father McGuckin preached. They requested further instruction and agreed to elect one of their chiefs as the Church representative. The missionary was impressed by their enthusiasm and saw "no reason to fear being able with God's help to make them pretty good Christians" — an optimistic assertion given the general reputation of the Chilcotin!

Three Chilcotin chiefs were known to Father McGuckin and he made interesting observations on them: Keogh, "a good man but a poor chief lacking energy and courage" but whom he felt would improve once the Durieu System was operating; Anaham, "a good chief, energetic and fearless" who kept his Indians in thorough subjection; and Alexis, who rated no comment other than he was "made Chief by Judge Cox in 1864." Father McGuckin appointed the "usual officers" of the Durieu System for Alexis' band and promised to do the same for the other two chiefs the following year if they would endeavour to have all their Indians assembled for that purpose. Again Father McGuckin exuded confidence as he wrote to his Bishop that although the work of Christianizing the Chilcotin would be "a little slow," patience and perseverance would succeed eventually."

With missionary work prospering, Father McGuckin persued another avenue of endeavour, the possibility of Indian education. The missionary intended to keep his promise to the Carrier Indians and provide education for their children. In addition, he had been distressed to find Indian girls living in the mining areas in a "deplorable state" and this led him to press for at least a school for girls. "In vain shall we teach the boys," he wrote to Bishop D'herbomez, "as long as the girls are ignorant and wicked." Since Catholic mothers were considered to be a mainstay of the Roman Catholic Church, Father McGuckin emphasized the desirability of Catholic Indian mothers; "to regenerate the Indians we should begin with the mothers of the future generation." While Father McGuckin's concern appears to have been religious training, his Bishop had something more practical in mind. In November 1868, D'herbomez wrote to the Superior General that he proposed to establish at St. Joseph's an industrial and agricultural school for the Indian children.[12]

The establishment of schools for Indian children had long been part of Oblate missionary work. Although in his *Constitution and Rules* Father de Mazenod refers only to Oblates teaching in "Minor Seminaries and Colleges," those in the mission field often had to undertake the teaching of Catholic and native children. When he established the British Columbia mainland's first mission in the Okanagan in 1859, Father Pandosy built a small school to accommodate both Indian and the few white children in the area. This day school was not a success. At that time, Indian parents could see little advantage for their children in reading and writing lessons. Consequently, when the children were not running away from the confines of the one-room school, they were being kept away by suspicious parents. Six months after the school opened, the Indians withdrew all the children after one was accidentally killed while in the care of the priest. In 1861, the Oblates decided that a boarding school would best suit their purpose, and they opened an industrial boarding school for Indian boys at St. Mary's Mission. Four years later Bishop D'herbomez requested an order of nuns, the Sisters of St. Ann, who since their arrival in the West in 1858 had established schools on Vancouver Island, to open schools for both Indians and whites at New Westminster, the Indian school to be supported by the Vicariate if necessary.[13] In view of Bishop D'herbomez's desire for Indian education at St. Joseph's, Father McGuckin's assurance that the surrounding Indians desired education for their children, the availability of space at the Mission house, and fertile land for the teaching of agriculture, a school for Indians was a logical move. In June 1869, while Bishop D'herbomez was in Europe and Father

Durieu had charge of affairs in Cariboo, Father Horris informed Father McGuckin that the Vicariate would sanction the opening of an Indian school for boys. The future of the Mission looked promising.

NOTES TO CHAPTER III

[1] Description of Richfield is taken from the *Cariboo Sentinal*, August 3, 1863.

[2] Unless otherwise indicated, quoted material is taken from the Correspondences of Father James Maria McGuckin, Oblate History, U.B.C.

[3] The *Cariboo Sentinal*, August 3, 1863.

[4] Father Charles Grandidier to Bishop D'herbomez, November 20, 1866, A.D.

[5] Dennis Murphy to Bishop D'herbomez, August 10, 1866, Oblate History, U.B.C.

[6] Minutes of the Vicariate Council, October 7/5, 1866, A.D.

[7] *Missions 1870*, pp. 87-108.

[8] Father Thomas, *Memoirs*, p. 14.

[9] Teit, "The Shuswap," p. 569.

[10] Report of the Vicariate written for the General Chapter in 1893, A.D.

[11] Father LeJacq to Superior General of Canada, October 21, 1895, Manuscript, O.A.

[12] *Missions*, 1870, pp. 87-108.

[13] Bishop D'herbomez to Sister Mary Providence, June 22, 1865, A.S.S.A.

Chapter IV

MISSIONARIES TO RANCHERS

"C'est immense" wrote Brother Blanchet of the Mission farm in May 1868, "il y a de quoi occuper six personnes." It does not take an understanding of French to realize that Brother Blanchet was somewhat dismayed at the amount of work he and Brother Surel were facing. St. Joseph's Mission had followed the pattern of other Oblate missions when the Bishop had purchased sufficient land to enable the missionaries to establish a self-supporting farm. In Oregon the Oblates had planted gardens around their missions, for often the Indians were starving and could not be relied upon to supply provisions for the missionaries. Unfortunately the land of the Yakima and Cayuse Indians was not very fertile and it was often an uphill struggle to maintain even the smallest garden. However, the Indians were encouraged to visit the missions' small holdings in the hope that they would be inspired to plant and nurture gardens for themselves.[1]

Father Pandosy who established the Oblates' first mission in British Columbia was also the first to plant fruit trees in the Okanagan Valley. He wrote enthusiastically to Bishop D'herbomez of the area's agricultural potential: "If Brother Blanchet is able to send us some vine cuttings, we shall be able to start a plantation."[2] Again the Oblates used their land to encourage the Indians. Historian Frank Buckland wrote of the Oblates' first years as Okanagan farmers, "they planted vines, fruit trees and garden seeds, with very little assistance from others to encourage them in their desire to teach the Indians husbandry as well as Christianity."[3] In using farms as models for the Indians, the Oblates adhered to the widely held belief that the Indian would become more civilized if he became a farmer. But, as Brother Blanchet's letter revealed, the Mission farm had grown far beyond a mere sustenance level and was much larger than was necessary as a teaching tool.

The Oblate Council had resolved to purchase up to 100 acres of land for the new mission, although 80 would have sufficed if the land had been relatively close to an Indian village. The land had to be irrigated, fertile enough to grow vegetables and wheat, and suitable for the rearing of animals.[4] Should the time come when Christianized Indians wished to live close to the Mission, the land would be available. Pomeroy's farm was particularly well adapted for the raising of stock, both cattle and horses, and the San José River which bordered the land could be used for irrigation. Government land surveyors had reported that green crops could be grown in abundance in the area, but it would take "intelligence in selecting the sites to raise hardier varieties of small grain and vegetables."[5]

Prospects looked good and Father McGuckin suggested that the Bishop enlarge their holdings.[6] As he understood it, the land had to be pre-empted in such a way "that the length did not exceed the breadth more than ⅓." Moreover, if the Bishop wanted to have the water rights, he would have to record and pre-empt 640 acres. This figure was the least that should be recorded for the Oblates would then have a "most valuable and most desirable property if ever the country became inhabited." Father McGuckin saw prospects for the Mission farm far beyond a self-supporting or educational basis. But, as the Bishop was not yet ready to invest in so much land, he purchased only the farm and, to keep within the law, pre-empted a further 160 acres. At the end of 1867, Father McGuckin informed Bishop D'herbomez that in the following year he intended to see thirty-eight acres planted in wheat, oats, barley, potatoes, turnips, peas and beans, and that these plans necessitated the services of another Brother as soon as possible.

The Irish Oblate was exceeding his authority in making plans for the Mission farm. Naturally, because he was English-speaking, he had dealt with the details of the farm purchase. He had researched the cost of hauling the lumber necessary to renovate the boundary house and finding that it was considerably cheaper both to have the wood hauled in winter and to leave the wood unhewed, he persuaded the Bishop to let him make the necessary arrangements. Labour costs were also cheaper in winter as with the shutdown of mining operations jobs became scarce. Father McGuckin was able to hire men to put up fencing for the Mission at fifty cents a day. He then hired a carpenter to remove the boundary house to a more central location and do any renovations necessary to make it suitable. His parishioners at Richfield raised the $200 necessary to haul down and put up the house, floor and line it, and to replace all doors and windows. Now that the Mission was running smoothly, Father McGuckin had his Richfield parish and the Carrier Indians of Alexandria and Quesnel to attend to. The running of the farm was initially in the hands of Father Jayol, then in the hands of Father LeJacq. But from the first the Irish Oblate had a vision of the farm as more than a provider for local needs, or a gathering place for Indians. He saw it as a source of income for both present and future missionary activities and as a sound financial base for the support of the Vicariate. He was quick to realize the potential of land in the Cariboo, and he wanted the Oblates to grasp the opportunity to develop and add to their holdings.

Apparently there were some who did not share the missionary's enthusiasm, for in a letter to the Bishop written in December 1867, the priest felt called upon to reply to criticism that had been levelled at his plans. He strongly argued the need to expand the farm's area in spite of the limited resources in manpower and money available in the Vicariate. He suggested that since St. Joseph's was "the best farm on the upper country and everything raised on it would meet with ready sale at the highest prices," it would be good business to send a lay Brother from another mission to work the land. If necessary, the Mission could pay two or three hundred dollars a year compensation to the donor mission to allow it to employ a replacement labourer. A Brother at St. Joseph's was well worth a thousand dollars a year because during the summer months the wages of labourers in the Cariboo were very high, and even the Indians refused to work "for less than a dollar per day."

Father McGuckin went on to defend his plans for enlarged agricultural activity at the Mission. To those Oblates who insisted that there was "no necessity for farming so much," the missionary had a ready and valid answer. If well-managed, the farm-ranch could support the already established schools at New Westminster and provide money for new schools at St. Joseph's and elsewhere. Each mission was expected to support the Vicariate's ecclesiastical programme as well as missionary endeavours. Of those Oblates who thought that collections among the settlers would suffice to meet these ends and obligations, Father McGuckin asked, "how could any person go to the settlers in the neighbourhood and ask for a subscription and at the same time have the best farm in the country lying waste?" Given the confidence of his fellow Oblates, and a reasonably free hand in the management of the land, the Irish missionary could see St. Joseph's becoming "the best spoke in the Procurator's wheel." Since the work of the Oblate Procurator was to deal directly with Rome, Father McGuckin obviously felt that the Mission would become something to boast of in high places!

Unfortunately for Father McGuckin's ambitious plans, Bishop D'herbomez had gone to Europe in 1869, leaving Paul Durieu in charge of the Vicariate. Durieu's priority was the conversion of the Indian and it was inevitable that he and Father McGuckin would not see eye to eye. Father McGuckin was not an enthusiastic Indian missionary. He made his share of visits to local Indian camps but when faced with extended tours, he suffered from "palpitations of the heart" and a variety of other mysterious ailments. In his opinion, "stinking salmon without salt and bread" left much to be desired! Consequently, when in early 1870 Father Durieu ordered him to make an extended circuit among the Babines in the Stuart Lake area, the Irish missionary tried, without success, to persuade his superior to send Father LeJacq. He pleaded that his presence was needed among the miners, but Father Durieu was unmoved.

The Richfield parish exhibited "boom and bust" characteristics. In the spring of 1869, Father McGuckin wrote enthusiastically of the past winter:

> My Congregation was larger than ever before, numbering from 40 to 50 every Sunday. There were 14 received Holy Communion on St. Patrick's Day and 27 on Easter Sunday. Three boys made their first Holy Communion and 5 men had the same happiness. Two of the latter were converts, one from the Church of England and the other from Presbyterians . . . I had a large number of Conversions of bad Catholics several of whom had been 15 to 30 years from their duty whilst there were others who made their first Confessions and Communions after having seen 40 "Snows."

By the fall, a large number of miners had left "to seek their fortune elsewhere" leaving the Oblate with a small congregation and the prospect of facing a lonely winter in Richfield. When Father Durieu insisted that Father McGuckin leave for Stuart Lake, a miraculous reversal apparently occurred. Since the miners had received "no additional encouraging news" of the new mines (the Omineca) "all the Caribooites" decided to remain where they were. The priest's congregation increased considerably and he offered as proof — since proof seemed necessary — the fact that "34 persons complied with their Easter duty." As "another proof," he was able to raise $400 for the Mission. In the face of such obvious generosity, the missionary felt obliged, "for the benefit of the Mission," to spend the summer in Cariboo. When Durieu remained implacable, Father McGuckin complained of his "poor state of health," but to no avail. In May, the Irish missionary left for the north and the Mission administration was left in the unwilling hands of Father LeJacq.

When, in the following spring, Father McGuckin next visited the Mission, he was appalled by the conditions he found. Like Durieu, Father LeJacq's only concern was the Indians. He had neither the time nor the inclination to be constantly keeping a state of order. What to Father McGuckin's eyes was total chaos, to Father LeJacq was most natural. To the Frenchman, there was more to life than cleaning and organizing the Mission House; to the Irishman life meant order and organization. "I have been told to my face," wrote the angry priest to his superior, "that it [the Mission house] is dirtier than a Si-wash's house, and I believe it to be true." As a further aggrevation for the Irish missionary, Father Durieu had sent no other Brother to help out, and the Mission was paying "a hired man high wages" to help Brother Surel put in the crop; "it annoys me very much to see how things have been and are still managed with regard to this mission."

The return of Bishop D'herbomez in May, ended the neglect at the Mission. Father McGuckin's enthusiasm always seemed to win over Bishop D'herbomez, and consequently, in early June, his lordship gave the missionary permission to pre-empt 400 acres adjoining the Mission ranch. At this time, Father McGuckin took out water rights for the Mission land for 100 years. A year later, "in consequence of the fences put up and about to be put up" by neighbouring ranchers, the Mission needed a greater amount of range for its cattle than it presently possessed. Father McGuckin suggested purchasing the Graham ranch which adjoined the Mission property. If the Oblates acquired it at the asking price of $400 it would be able to provide "for any amount of stock" that the Mission was ever likely to possess. The Bishop was slow to answer his missionary, but, confident that the reply would be positive, Father McGuckin took responsibility upon himself and bought the property.

By this time, Father McGuckin was facing the prospect of opening a school, and the development of the farm into a ranch neces-

sitated either more Oblate Brothers or hired men to do the extra work. As the Vicariate was continually expanding and the number of Oblates was still relatively few, more Brothers were out of the question, and as usual Father McGuckin was opposed to paying local help. In an attempt to relieve the situation, in the summer of 1872 the Irish missionary involved the Mission in a partnership deal. He explained to the Bishop:

> In this section, Farmers sometimes let their farms to be worked as *shares*. Here are generally the conditions: the Proprietor supplies the land, teams, implements and half the seeds. The Contractor feeds and takes care of the teams, ploughs, sows, reaps, thrashes, in a word does all the labour and pays all expense until the Grain is put in the Granery when it is equally divided between two parties. But all the straw remains with the Proprietor. The Contractor also has to give half the seed.

By such a contract, Father McGuckin expected the Oblates to be "delivered from all the trouble and expense" and, with a larger area sown in wheat, the Mission would have "a larger return than at present." He also hoped to exchange part of the straw for work on fences and ditches.

Trusting to Father McGuckin's business acumen, the Bishop agreed that, if a suitable partner could be found, the Mission could make such an arrangement. In August 1872, a five-year agreement was drawn up between the Mission and Edward Shearer, a "steady, sober, honest Catholic" who had taken an interest in the proposal and had "sufficient means to undertake it." Shearer agreed, in exchange for the terms explained by Father McGuckin plus "five yearling heifers and four heifer calves," to put in 70 acres of each crop, wheat, barley, and oats, to keep all equipment in good repair, as well as fences, ditches and dams; to cut, haul, and put up new fences (including splitting 10,000 rails); to clear all the land covered in willow (at his own expense) and sow the same in Timothy hay. In additional clauses, agreed upon a month later, Shearer was to furnish the Mission each year with 250 lbs. of "good, fresh butter" providing that the Oblates kept at least 24 milk cows on the ranch. To keep the Mission's side of the bargain, Father McGuckin requested a dozen milk cows from the Okanagan Mission.

The Irish Oblate felt confident that he had struck a profitable bargain. Shearer promised to expand the planted acreage the following year to 100 acres of each crop and the missionary "had no doubt" that he would accomplish it. The bargain appeared to free the missionaries from extensive farm and ranch work. In October, confident of future prosperity, Father McGuckin agreed, with the Bishop's approval, to purchase another property adjoining the Mission. A rancher named Bates, who had already bought all the land that lay alongside the available property, was also interested in purchasing more land. If he had succeeded in obtaining the available property, he would have erected fences which would have prevented the Mission stock from reaching good grazing land. Consequently the Oblates considered it a necessary purchase. With land enough for their stock and a good man in charge of the ranch, the missionaries could contemplate an orderly and profitable period. Unfortunately, that winter, events did not progress smoothly for Mr. Shearer. All the horses got distemper and, though none died, they were considerably weakened. This "annoyed Shearer considerably" but he faced another graver problem. He "had a dispute" with a man he had hired. The matter went to the Court at Richfield and Shearer lost approximately $400. This had a "serious effect on his purse" and he began to talk of leaving farming.

By April, the "steady, sober, honest Catholic" had become "a regular tyrant." He had quarrelled with the Oblates and, in defiance of their wishes, he had forcibly taken possession of the cabin on what had been the Graham property. There was talk of legal action, but things were smoothed over when Shearer agreed to sow 25 acres of the Graham land in grain and seed in exchange for the accommodation. Unfortunately the arrival of a new missionary, Father Charles Marchal, provoked more serious trouble. Shearer and Father Marchal took an instant dislike to one another and quarrelled at every given opportunity. Several times their heated disputes almost resulted in physical violence. It may have been simply a clash of personalities, but Father Marchal was a man who enjoyed carpentry and, when he was at the Mission, he liked to build and repair wherever necessary. It is possible that he and Shearer clashed over what the farmer could term interference in his work.

In June, Father McGuckin was summoned to attend the Assizes at Quesnel to prove the legality of a marriage between a French Canadian and an Indian woman. Satisfied to see Judge Baillie Begbie give the local population "a good lesson" by sentencing some white men to six months imprisonment "for interfering with married women who are Indians," the priest returned to the Mission to find a "scandalous" situation. Another quarrel between Shearer and Father Marchal had resulted finally in a physical battle. The farmer had pushed the missionary into a ditch and the missionary had struck Shearer with a shovel. At one point Shearer had threatened to shoot the priest. It became obvious that one of the two would have to go and the farmer was considered more expendable. Unfortunately, Shearer's contract had still four years to run. The Oblates tried to settle the matter out-of-court but the farmer refused. He declared that he would remain on the Graham ranch until he got a fair settlement.

The Bishop was afraid that a lawsuit would cause a scandal, but the dispute had already become a scandal in the district. In September, the matter went to court. With Judge Begbie presiding, Mr. Alexander E. B. Davie (future Premier) appearing for the Oblates and Mr. George Walkem (future Premier) appearing for Shearer, the case went to arbitration. Dennis Murphy, representing the Oblates, and John Sawyer representing Shearer agreed on all matters but one. Sawyer asked $800 compensation as Shearer was giving up his four-year lease. Murphy refused, and the matter went to the umpire, Mr. Oliver Howe, Government Agent at Quesnel. He agreed with Sawyer and awarded the $800. Although the Oblates felt the decision unjust and Mr. Davie advised an appeal, the Bishop decided that enough scandal had been caused and he accepted the settlement. It was an expensive and embarrassing lesson for Father McGuckin, even though neighbours promised help with the work left unfinished by Shearer.

Shearer owed $1600 to the Oppenheimer brothers and he gave his award to them in part payment. David Oppenheimer called at the Mission to collect the $800 and Father McGuckin was forced to borrow from the Vicariate fund. Father Horris, the burser, must have relished the situation as Father McGuckin had frequently scorned him for his cautious attitude towards money. Still believing that Shearer owed some money to the Mission, Father McGuckin delayed payment of the $800 and to add to his discomfort the Oppenheimers threatened to put the matter in the hands of the sheriff. Father McGuckin's attempt to lift the burden of agricultural work from the missionaries had failed. From this time on the Oblates would be farmers, ranchers and, when necessary, cowboys.

For several years, the Oblates maintained their property, gradually increasing their crop acreage and their stock. In 1880, another farm adjoining the Mission land and owned by a Mr. Messier came on the market when its owner decided to leave for the

United States. He offered his farm for $200 and Father McGuckin appealed once more to the Bishop:

We have unanimously agreed to ask your Lordship's permission to be allowed to purchase it. Principally on account of the water, which, whoever wins the farm, has the right of carrying through our ditch. . . . Of course the land would be very useful too as for grazing etc. There are rails enough on it to fence it. We are willing to sacrifice other necessary wants in order to have it and prevent a Chinaman or some other from having it.

This need to prevent "undesirable neighbours" from encircling or in any way affecting mission land caused another claustrophobic reaction a year later when the Oblate Superior was informed that five pre-emption claims had been taken up "between the Graham place at the Rocky Point and the 150 Mile House." The Mission cattle had increased beyond what had earlier been anticipated and as each head of cattle required about ten acres of range for sustenance, more grazing land was required.[7] Only the "first flat" between the Mission ranch and the Felker farm now remained unoccupied, and the Mission staked off 320 acres of this flat to ensure grazing for its cattle. This land was officially pre-empted in August, 1881. Each time the Mission requested more land, the Oblate Council allowed the purchase. The only available land that the Mission did not want to touch was that considered Indian land. Father McGuckin's reason was more practical than altruistic. He felt that it would be "too much trouble" to dispossess the Indians. By 1881, the ranch amounted to 1600 acres.

A combination of good management and good husbandry created a highly successful enterprise. Between 1870 and 1885 most of the large cattle ranches in the Cariboo reached their maximum, or close to their maximum growth,[8] and the Mission was no exception. The Oblates were steadily expanding their herd and improving the quality of their horses. It was a matter of some pride when in the spring of 1872, a Mission mare gave birth to a colt "exactly 13 hands high," the largest ever known in that part of the country.

Whenever Father McGuckin acquired new property, he made a good bargain. In obtaining the Graham ranch, the Oblates acquired in addition to the land, "a barn, cabin, dairy, a good deal of fencing, a wagon worth $100, a good plough, harrow, a good roller, irrigator, wheelbarrow, grain cradle, 2 scythes, neck yoke, 2 hay forks, 2 rakes, and a good sleigh." Messier's farm had gained the Mission more control over the water supply, and the 1881 pre-emption had secured an adequate amount of grazing land for the increasing herd. But adding extra acres did not in itself assure a profitable enterprise. The amount of land that changed hands illustrates the precarious nature of farming and ranching during those pioneer years. Although subjected to all the sudden reversals of weather conditions, market fluctuations, and the often unstable economy of the developing province, the Oblates' good management helped them to survive.

There were years when a glut of cattle, or an over-abundance of certain crops, severely affected prices. In the fall of 1873, the price for grain dropped sharply from five cents per pound to two and a half cents. Fortunately Father McGuckin had managed to sell 5,000 lbs. to Mr. Bates before the price fell, and he planned to exchange the rest, approximately 11,000 lbs., for "flour, seed, and horsefeed." Often when there was little cash available crops were exchanged for provisions, building materials, even labour. Although there were years when even Father McGuckin's enthusiasm waned — in 1880 he considered selling the Mission horses, "all good stock," because of the expense of feeding them through a particularly severe winter — the ranch continued to develop and more than hold its own among competitive neighbours.

In 1874, when extremely wet weather caused most farmers to lose their crops, the Mission "in spite of wet weather and want of help" produced an abundant crop "of first quality." In the exceptionally severe winter of 1879-1880, the temperature fell to -50°F. This was very hard on the stock. As the severe weather continued into late February, many of the ranchers lost a large number of cattle and the Indians lost a good number of their horses. The Mission stock was more fortunate. The Oblates lost four calves, and several young cows were left "poor and weak," but the greatest percentage of the herd survived because they had "plenty of fodder and pretty good shelter." The cold winter was followed by floods, and it was May before ploughing could begin. The water prevented the farmers from planting spring wheat but the Oblates had had the foresight to sow "the only Fall wheat sown in the neighbourhood."

As Father McGuckin had foreseen, the Mission farm-ranch proved to be a valuable asset to the Vicariate. From 1876 onwards, the sale of farm produce made it possible for St. Joseph's to contribute $850 annually towards the cost of the Mission schools. Whenever the Sisters of St. Ann[9] were in financial difficulties at the girls' school, the Oblates donated some of the farm crops to assist them. In 1887, for example, Father McGuckin supplied them with between 2500 and 3000 lbs. of wheat. He considered it a practical move to give them supplies instead of cash because, since the Sisters were so well thought of in the community, they were likely to obtain a better price for their goods. In spite of Father McGuckin's protests, the Mission came to the financial aid of St. Louis Mission, Kamloops. The Irish Oblate thought that it was throwing good money after bad to support a mission that was in financial straits simply through bad management, but at least he was able to see St. Joseph's provide the service he had anticipated in 1867. In the Report of the Vicariate to Rome in 1918, the Oblates wrote: "St. Joseph's Mission has been for many years and still is the principal support of the Vicariate thanks to the possession of tractable land and to the administration of those who have been and still are in charge."

NOTES TO CHAPTER IV

[1] Lardon, "O.M.I. on the Parific Coast," p. 16.

[2] *Missions, 1870*, p. 307.

[3] Kay Cronin, *Cross in the Wilderness*, Vancouver, 1959, p. 67.

[4] Deliberations du Conseil Provincial, October 1866, A.D.

[5] Abstracts from Reports on Cariboo District made by British Columbia Land Surveyors to the Department of Lands, 1891-1927, King's Printer, P.A.B.C., p. 99. Cited hereafter as Reports on Cariboo District.

[6] Unless otherwise indicated quoted material is from Father McGuckin's correspondence.

[7] Reports on Cariboo District, p. 53.

[8] Thomas R. Weir, *Ranching: The Southern Interior Plateau of British Columbia*, Geographical Branch Memoir 4, Queen's Printer, 1955, p. 56.

[9] This refers to the Sisters of St. Ann who were at St. Joseph's. See Chapter V.

Chapter V

A NEW DIRECTION

When the decision was made to establish an Indian school at the Mission, Father McGuckin, in spite of his earlier enthusiasm for Indian education, reacted with alarm. In a letter to the Bursar he made it clear that he expected "a double school" at St. Joseph's, one for the Indian children and one for the white. He looked upon this as so necessary that he never considered "opposition from headquarters."[1] Durieu's decision to go ahead with Indian education had placed Father McGuckin in a dilemma. In addition to his promise to the Indians, he had promised a school also to the parents of white children and unfortunately, the Vicariate was not financially strong enough to support both.

When the Oblates took upon themselves the sole responsibility for the development of the Vicariate, they took on a tremendously expensive task. Some money was available from the Society for the Propagation of the Faith but new missionary areas were expected to become self-sufficient as quickly as possible. The white Catholic population was expected to contribute generously to new developments and one of the priests' tasks was fund-raising. In 1863, for example, when a new church was needed for the benefit of French, French-Canadian, Spanish and Italian-speaking Catholics of the Victoria area, Father McGuckin, revealing a natural talent for fund-raising, persuaded many English-speaking Catholics, and several Protestants, to contribute to the building fund. Consequently, early in 1865, the Oblates opened St. Louis Church, next to the College. Churches were considered essential but the Catholic Church had always given the highest priority to parochial education for its young. In British Columbia there was an added urgency as Bishop D'herbomez anxiously regarded the spread of Protestant schools. In August 1862 the Reverend R. Jameson, a Presbyterian minister, opened a non-denominational school in New Westminster to accommodate any parents wishing private education for their children. Eight months later, under the direction of Mr. James McIlveen, the first public school opened.[2] Paying pupils were an important source of income and consequently there was urgency in Bishop D'herbomez's letters to the Sisters of St. Ann pressing for them to open a school for girls in New Westminster. The Bishop wrote that Bishop Hill had just announced that "a lady was going to open a Collegiate School in the city" and that haste was necessary "to prevent Protestant schools from gaining ground."[3] By the end of June 1865, the Sisters had opened a school for white paying pupils and non-paying Indian children in a convent that the Bishop had prepared for them. Simultaneously, St. Louis College was transferred from Victoria to New Westminster, its upkeep now in the hands of the Oblates. When an Indian school was opened at St. Mary's Mission more funding had to be found.

To obtain the finances necessary for the upkeep and continuation of educational developments within the Vicariate, Bishop D'herbomez requested his priests to make collections among white Catholics. Father McGuckin had complied and, in a little over a year, the Irish Oblate had collected twenty-two hundred dollars in donations for the Church from both miners and settlers. In addition, the Catholic congregation had subscribed to the purchase of Deputy Sheriff Lee's house which adjoined the church. Sheriff Lee was returning to California and the only offer he had received for his house was from "a band of Chinamen who had a mining claim convenient to the house." Since the church had already been put in danger of burning down from several fires in Mr. Lee's house, Father McGuckin did not want the Chinese to buy it but had neither money nor authorization to prevent the sale. Two Frenchmen, Monsieur Lallier and Captain Trahillet, collected sufficient money to purchase the house and it was donated to the Church. But Father McGuckin was well aware that neither money nor house had been donated unconditionally. While they appreciated the Oblate's efforts to give some schooling to their children, the people of the mining district were no more receptive of makeshift educational facilities than they were of makeshift religious opportunities. For a while, Father McGuckin was able to persuade Catholic parents to send at least their older children to the schools in New Westminster but the reluctance of the parents to send their children so far from home can be exemplified in Father McGuckin's exhortation to Father Horris that he make George Vijnsko write to his mother "very constantly." Soon these parents began to pressure for the establishment of a local Catholic school, and Father McGuckin was most sympathetic to their cause.

Although, unlike his Bishop, Father McGuckin had not experienced active Protestant animosity (although the Orange Order did establish a lodge in Richfield), his upbringing in Northern Ireland had instilled in him a strong antipathy to the English Protestants. He too felt that the Oblates should do all in their power not only to counteract the spread of Protestant schools, but also to establish a firm financial base for the Church, which would enable it to spread and develop quickly. He reminded Bishop D'herbomez of the important financial support supplied by Cariboo's Catholics and urged him to carry out the work of educating the Cariboo children without delay: "the people in subscribing so generously in these hard times will demand as much generosity on our part, and will expect to see their money put to good purpose."

When, in D'herbomez's absence, the Indian school appeared to be getting priority, the Irish Oblate made it clear that the Oblates were making an error. He stated categorically that the people of Cariboo would not support such a school. Although the miners had sent money to support the orphan Indians kept by the Sisters of St. Ann at New Westminster, they would not subscribe for local Indians; "mark well this difference" he warned, "if you have nothing but an Indian school at St. Joseph's never calculate in raising a subscription towards supporting it." Moreover the settlers certainly could not be expected to subscribe for Indian education, Father McGuckin argued, if the Bishop refused to educate their children for payment.

Father McGuckin's concern for the future prosperity of the Church was revealed clearly as he enumerated the reasons why the white Catholic population should be accommodated: "as true representatives and Apostles in this New Country of our Holy Religion the Oblates should provide education for orphans and children of white parents as well as of the natives"; the school at St. Joseph's could act as a "feeder" for those in New Westminster, ensuring their continued prosperity; "half-breeds" whose fathers were "generally able and willing to give a helping hand in the carrying out of holy and great undertakings" could be accommodated; all the children in the area who would be given the opportunity through education to play a "major role" in the development of the Province would be "raised and educated as Catholics"; the school would be fully supported without cost to the Vicariate and would be seen as tangible evidence that the two thousand dollars now collected by Father McGuckin for school purposes was being put to good use; the Oblates had "the sympathy and support of all or nearly all the inhabitants from Clinton to Barkerville" but, "owing to the slow movements of Superiors," their patience was nearly exhausted; finally, a familiar theme, the Protestants were now making efforts to establish a school on Williams Creek and some were negotiating with Bishop Hill to obtain the services of a minister. "Experience should teach you" concluded Father McGuckin, "to take firm possession of *all* before these scourges arrive."

In spite of Father McGuckin's logic, and possibly because of the Bishop's absence, the school question was left in abeyance until December the following year. At that time a meeting of concerned parents at Richfield petitioned Governor Anthony Musgrave to establish a school district in the area. Father McGuckin wrote in haste to Paul Durieu; "now what is to be done? Of the 16 or 17 children belonging to Williams Creek about 12 of them are Catholics. Shall all of these go to the Common School?" Using his abundant business acumen which he had already used to establish a night school and library for the miners, the Irish Oblate went on to suggest a plan that would satisfy Catholic parents and be a good deal for the Vicariate. Feeling that the parents of non-Catholic children would not object to a Catholic teacher, he proposed that all parents should be persuaded to sign a petition urging the Governor to appoint him as local teacher under the terms of legislation passed in 1869.[4] The house adjoining the church that the local Catholics had purchased for their priest could serve as the school. An added attraction for a Vicariate ever in need of funds was the salary of "approximately $1000 per annum" that the teacher would receive.

Two weeks after receiving Father McGuckin's letter, Father Durieu and the Vicariate Council discussed the developing situation and Father McGuckin's solution. They decided that they could not authorize Father McGuckin to take charge of a Common School at Richfield, however, they resolved that a school for white boys would be opened at St. Joseph's Mission and that a lay Brother would be sent as teacher.[5] The school was to open in September 1871 with Father McGuckin in charge. In June 1871, Bishop D'herbomez returned from Europe to face the suggestions of both Father McGuckin and Father LeJacq that the best interests of the children would be served if the school was taken out of their busy hands and placed in the hands of the Sisters of St. Ann.

Bishop D'herbomez shared the concerns of his missionaries. His Oblates were already engaged in parochial as well as missionary duties and he could spare no more as teachers. Once again the school question was temporarily shelved until, in June 1872, the Bishop informed Father McGuckin, whom he appointed the new Superior of St. Joseph's, that as soon as a combined convent and school was built, he would send three Sisters to take charge of education at the Mission. Father McGuckin lost no time in spreading the good news and, as the people "were most anxious to see the school opened," they contributed to a collection taken up by Dennis Murphy and Mr. Dunlevy of Soda Creek for the completion of the new building. "I am pretty certain that the Sisters will have children enough to keep them busy," wrote the priest, "I think they should make every effort to open the school in May." When, by May, the Sisters had not yet arrived, Father McGuckin suggested that the Sisters should advertise in the *Cariboo Sentinel* "to give a proof of the opening of the school as . . . there are some people incredulous on this point." The Bishop however was experiencing difficulties with the Sisters of St. Ann which would cause both he and Father McGuckin distress for three more years.

When the Sisters of St. Ann had answered Bishop D'herbomez's request for nuns to run schools established in his Vicariate, they agreed to provide Sisters for schools as the development of missions and the immigration of settlers warranted it.[6] Consequently, in February 1873, the Bishop confidently addressed himself to Mother Mary Eulalie, Superior General of the Sisters of St. Ann in Lachine, Quebec, on the topic of the new convent/school being built for the Sisters at St. Joseph's Mission. He explained that the building was now nearing completion and was one of the largest of its kind in the interior. It had two separate wings, a boarding school area for girls, and a second for "les petits garçons." The Sisters' rooms were situated between the two wings. The Bishop stressed that it was necessary to send two Sisters capable of teaching school in English since the government wished all children to be taught in English.[7] The reply to his request was not encouraging. The Sisters had no personnel available to undertake a new establishment and Bishop D'herbomez was forced to consider asking other orders to undertake the work.

In June, Father Durieu took the place of his ailing Bishop at the General Chapter of the Oblates in Paris where he was officially made co-adjuter for the Vicariate. This appointment made Father Durieu Bishop D'herbomez's successor and consequently he was made honourary bishop with the title Bishop of Marcopolis.[8] On his return to Canada in October he visited the Sisters of St. Ann at Lachine pleading the cause of his bishop. Back in New Westminster he wrote on behalf of Bishop D'herbomez to Lachine and again reiterated what was required of the nuns in the Vicariate. Durieu's version, however, was somewhat different than the Bishop's. He wrote that St. Joseph's required five Sisters by the end of April 1874 because the school would have *three* sections: one for boys under eight years of age; a second for young girls, the children of white parents, and a third for Indian girls. Father Durieu was still determined on an Indian school!

Again the importance of haste was stressed because the schools of "atheists and protestants" were multiplying everywhere. And, Durieu assured the Sister Superior, Bishop D'herbomez regarded as his most important work the opening, in each mission district, schools where children "des blancs que des sauvages" could receive an education that conformed with the principles of Catholicism.[9] In spite of a reiteration by Father Durieu that the Bishop would be forced to find another congregation of Sisters to teach the young girls of the Vicariate, at its December 1873 meeting, the Council of the Sisters of St. Ann decided that their community could not accept the school at St. Joseph's. They did not have sufficient Sisters for work which was going to require a large number of nuns for many years.[10]

Although Bishop D'herbomez was willing to find a replacement order, it would take time, and events in the Cariboo made the immediate opening of the school absolutely necessary. Paul Durieu was correct when he spoke of the spread of non-Catholic schools. In 1873, the building of a boarding and day school commenced at Cache Creek; the school formally opened on June 2, 1874. Within one month the school had thirty-six pupils — as many as the building could accommodate. According to British Columbia's first School Act passed on May 15, 1865, all Common schools were to be conducted upon non-sectarian principles; "all books of a Religious character teaching Denominational dogma were strictly excluded." However, clergymen of any denomination could visit the school before and after regular school hours to give religious instruction to the children of their denomination.[11] Because of the initial success of the school, the Superintendent of Education recommended that a second such institute be erected at Soda Creek.

Meanwhile, as could be expected, Father McGuckin was losing all patience. The prospect of losing possible pupils to the Common schools, and the embarrassment of continual delay in the arrival of the Sisters, provoked the missionary to write in anger to his Bishop:

I am very much annoyed at not having learned anything definite about the Sisters. If they are not coming, I think I may clear out of this part of the Country, for it is almost unbearable the complaints the people are making about their not having come ere this.

When this outburst brought no favourable reply, Father McGuckin decided to take matters into his own hands and open at least a boys' school at the Mission. In December he informed Bishop D'herbomez that he intended opening the school on December 9th, and that he would do his best "to give it a good name to begin with." Although the school opened before completion of the Cache Creek school, it looked for a time as if the Oblates had left it too late. The economy of the Cariboo was as precarious as most farming-ranching areas and, as 1873 was a bad year for selling farming produce and cattle, cash was in short supply. When the Mission school opened, only four boarders and three half-boarders presented themselves, with two boarders arriving the following week. Father McGuckin remained optimistic however, blaming the small number on the "severe winter" and anticipating fifteen to twenty when spring arrived. His letter to the Bishop reveals the importance Father McGuckin placed on the school:

The boys I have received have all, except one, to commence ABC. And six of them to learn the Lord's prayer, although one of the last mentioned is 13 years old and 2 others 11 years old each. I think it is time to gather such as these in School. Nevertheless these are the boys that will shortly hold the first place in Society in this Section of the Country. They will be all ours if we only can manage to educate them under our care. At present Your Lordship is aware that dull times are not encouraging to carrying on School, nevertheless the parents here will pay for their Children provided we are in a position to accept what they can give us. That is they will make their payments partly in cash and partly in Cattle and provisions. I think it will soon be necessary to have both boys' and Girls' Schools. . . . If I was sure that you would send the Sisters I would be delivered of much anxiety for the School must be kept open and be attended to if we are not to see all our Catholic Children grow up Infidals or go to the Common School.

In spite of the uncertain beginning, the development of the school was most gratifying. The priests and lay Brothers were educated men, and even non-Catholics appreciated the quality of the education offered by the Mission. The boarding school at St. Joseph's was soon filled to capacity and Father McGuckin requested both additional teaching help and classroom space. In less than a year, boys were attending from all parts of the Cariboo. In September 1874, five boys were sent down from Stuart Lake, and several more were expected. In addition, two boarders from the Cache Creek school moved to St. Joseph's and the priest was promised "ten more that had been at the same Institute last year." This movement of boys from Cache Creek was of course a most gratifying event. The reputation of the school grew and pupils even from distant Victoria attended.

If the boys' school was flourishing, the lack of a girls' school was causing Father McGuckin continued distress. There was no way that the Oblates could conceive of establishing a school to accommodate both boys and girls; within the Catholic Church the idea of mixed classes was anethema. Until the Sisters arrived only one girl had received any schooling at the Mission and it was not a happy situation for Father McGuckin. In 1874, three children of the Felker family were half-boarders at the school, including one daughter aged about ten or twelve whom the Oblate had permitted to attend the school with her brothers since, he claimed, both she and her brothers were "ignorant of the first notions of their religion." While the girl "advanced rapidly in secular and religious knowledge," she also advanced into womanhood — at least too much so for Father McGuckin's peace of mind. A child among a group of boys was one thing; a developing teenager was another! When Father McGuckin refused to take her back after the summer vacation, her mother threatened to send the girl to the Common school. Thus Father McGuckin was forced to ask the Bishop's permission to continue giving her lessons.

When pleading, as he continually did, for the nuns to open a girls' school, Father McGuckin constantly referred to the only alternative offered to Roman Catholic parents, Mme. Petiteau's "den of infamy" at Cache Creek:

> There are upwards of 30 pupils in the common school . . . boys and girls, up to fourteen years old, all eat, study, play and sleep together in the same apartments. Could a more diabolical institution be established for ruining the Children of the Country?

He charged that girls baptized by the missionaries stood in danger of becoming prostitutes if forced to attend the school. In August 1874, the priest's expectations of a crisis situation were realized when a fourteen-year-old Catholic girl, whose father had been waiting "year after year" for the opening of a Catholic girls' school, was expelled "for immorality."

When eight more months passed without any action, Father McGuckin once more vented his anger in a letter to Bishop D'herbomez in which he accused the Bishops of Victoria and Oregon, the Sisters of St. Ann, and even Father Durieu, of preventing the Bishop from obtaining the help of other religious orders. Throwing away any of the restraint with which he should have approached his Superior, Father McGuckin continued his attack:

> Permit me, My Lord, to transcribe for you the words that our Holy Father addressed lately to the Archbishop of Rheims: — 'I could easily support my own sorrow, and even the trouble of the Church, but when I see them drag from me the Children, the poor little Children, and give them an infidal education it breaks my heart.' . . . This very same misfortune is happening here to children who have been baptized by us and whose parents subscribed liberally towards the building of a house for the Sisters. Is it any wonder now that those parents say we raised money under false pretences and that the Sisters of Victoria are only humbugging you?

Wishing himself "a thousand miles away" because of the "false and ridiculous" position his Superior had placed him in, Father McGuckin warned that if a second Common school opened at Soda Creek it was pointless for any nuns to go to St. Joseph's. "The foothold that we have worked so hard and sacrificed so much to obtain in this section," he finished, "will be lost and the rising generation with it."

The Bishop may have been angered by his subordinate's blunt words, but he heeded Father McGuckin's warning. He wrote to the Sisters of Providence who were established in Oregon and, simultaneously, he requested Father McGuckin whose cousin was a Sister of the Presentation in Gragheald, Ireland, to write to the Order to see if they would be interested in the work. As a result of this correspondence, three Sisters of Providence arrived at St. Joseph's in September 1875, and in November the Presentations offered nuns for the Mission.

The Sisters of Providence were delighted with everything they saw at St. Joseph's. On condition that they could be "sole and absolute proprietors" of the convent plus ten to twenty acres of land, they proposed, if approval could be obtained from the Mother Superior in Quebec, to open an orphanage and boarding and day school "for white and half-breed girls." The Sisters made it clear however that the Indian work would be their primary concern, with the white school secondary and "as a means of carrying out the works of Charity." In their letter, the Sisters of the Presentation offered to take on the role of teaching "the whites, half-breeds and Indians" but, "as part of the bargain," they desired Father McGuckin to travel to Ireland for the Sisters.

In spite of these generous offers, both of which would have complemented Indian missionary activity, neither Order took on the work at the Mission. In January 1876, Father McGuckin received an apologetic letter from Sister Peter, one of the nuns who had visited St. Joseph's. Reverend Mother General had written that it was impossible for her to send Sisters to St. Joseph's. On February 23, at a Provincial Council meeting, the Oblates decided they must reject the offer of the Presentations as they were a cloistered order and would require special attention.[12] Perhaps because of the Bishop's determination to counterbalance "the pernicious influence" of the Common schools, the Sisters of St. Ann finally relented. In September 1876, Mother Mary Eulalie, General Superior, and Sister Marie Hélène, Assistant General, who were in British Columbia for the official opening of St. Joseph's Hospital, Victoria (Victoria General), accompanied Sisters Marie Clement, Marie Joachim and Marie Octavie on their journey to St. Joseph's Mission.

Unlike the Sisters of Providence, Mother Mary Eulalie was not impressed by the aspect of St. Joseph's Mission. The journey itself had been miserable enough. One of the young Sisters wrote to her own sister in Victoria: "I hope I shall not see you again for a long time. I love you too much to have you undertake this terrible journey for my sake and I don't love you enough to undertake it again for yours."[13] In spite of the warm welcome of Father McGuckin, and Indian missionary Father Charles Marchal (Father LeJacq had gone to Stuart Lake in 1873), the isolation of the Mission caused the Superior General to have misgivings. She was quite willing, if the Sisters so desired, to return the nuns to Victoria. The young Sisters wished to remain however and their Superior reluctantly agreed to leave them. In the combined convent/school building — purchased along with twelve acres of land from the Oblates — "about 110′ x 30′, situated upon the side of a mountain, opposite the Father Oblates' School," the Sisters began twelve years of teaching. Their pupils who were the children of ranchers, miners, French-Canadians, and Catholic Indian mothers married to white men, were "in general bright and willing to work." The Oblates "looked after the interests" of the Sisters' school in regards to provisions and heating, and the Sisters reciprocated by having their girls wash, iron, mend, and do other kinds of sewing for the boys' school.[14]

For a number of years both schools received approximately thirty and forty children each. Because Bishop D'herbomez desired the Oblate school to succeed he allowed four Oblate priests for the Mission, three for teaching in the School. Since the schools were primarily boarding schools, the children needed supervision twenty-four hours a day and, when they were not in class, they were watched by a lay brother. Although the Oblate school advertised "a thorough English and Commercial education," the boys were taught also all aspects of farming and ranching. Similarly the girls were taught how to be good housewives. Some parents, although they paid full fees for their children, desired their sons to do physical work three or four hours a day so that their children, who would most likely earn their living from the land, "might learn to do something more than reading and writing." In addition some boys and girls whose parents were having difficulty finding their fees, worked to pay for their schooling. In February 1878, Father McGuckin asked the Bishop to send another Brother to the Mission for the express purpose of teaching boys the "rudiments of husbandry." This proved to be a mixed blessing however as the boys had to be constantly supervised while training and often created problems by their inefficiency or laziness.

During summer vacation often a dozen or more boys and girls remained at the schools and had to be cared for. Father McGuckin who was both principal and teacher began to complain to Bishop D'herbomez concerning the pressures of his work:

> Our vacation commenced on the 25th inst. and still 15 boarders will spend their vacation with me and probably more will arrive in a week or two; so you may easily imagine my free time for my other duties. It is only while they are in bed that I can find time to attend to other things.

In spite of the time already devoted to the school, in 1877, the Bishops introduced another area of education at St. Joseph's. Several young men had expressed a desire to join the Oblate order and St. Joseph's was to be used as a preparatory school for them. They were taught Latin and theology by the experienced priests teaching there. Michael Hanley, "who desired very much to become a priest," was sent by the Bishop from New Westminster as early as 1874. In January 1877, Father McGuckin asked the Bishop's permission to allow several pupils who were "anxious to commence studies for the Priesthood" to begin their Latin studies without delay. The Bishop acquiesced but the young men, whose families were not able to afford the cost of their further studies, were expected to assist in the school during the year or two they spent in theological study. In spite of this help, Father McGuckin felt the need for still more assistance. To this end, he wrote to a friend in Ireland offering to pay the passage — with the Bishop's consent — of any young men who desired to become priests but who lacked the finances to acquire the necessary education. By this means, he obtained the services of a Mr. James McBride. In 1882, William Murphy of Lac La Hache (the son of Dennis Murphy), who received his early education at the Mission, became the first native son of the Cariboo to be ordained an Oblate.

Although both schools succeeded very well, especially with regard to "the amount of good done," and the academic and religious instruction imported to the rising generation of whites and Métis who attended them, they were scarcely, at any time, paying institutions. The uncertainty that accompanied the early years of agricultural developments in the Cariboo, such as adjustments to severe weather conditions, fluctuating markets, and the inexperience of many farmers and ranchers, led to years of financial difficulty. In some years when the parents of children had insufficient means to pay their fees, the Mission was obliged to assist the Sisters by providing total sustenance for them and their charges. To have turned the children away would have been tantamount to pushing them into government schools, and consequently many unusual offers were accepted in lieu of money. For example, Mr. Charles Eagle, who had two daughters in the school "and others growing," offered to build an addition to the over-crowded convent as payment for schooling. By April 1880, the total amount of unpaid fees for both schools was $7,000 but, in spite of his belief that the future held out "little hope of improvement," Father McGuckin insisted that it was not prudent to close the schools even in the face of such financial difficulty "lest the Protestants or government would take advantage of it to open one of their own."

After the Oblates opened a boys' school at Kamloops in 1880, the numbers of boys at St. Joseph's declined until by 1888 there were only nine or ten applications. A similar situation existed in the girls' school. From 1886 to 1888 the Sisters, only two of whom were now at the school, maintained between twenty and thirty girls but only twelve were expected to return the next year. Many of the girls had been orphans living on the Sisters' charity and, as the Sisters' debt increased, they were forced to accept paying pupils only. These were too few to warrant continuing the school. Asked why the Sisters left a place "so rich in sacrifices," Sister Mary Infant Jesus, a former teacher at the Mission, replied: "I think we left because there were not enough children to maintain the school and we could not live on sacrifices alone."[15] Both schools closed in 1888.

NOTES TO CHAPTER V

[1] Unless otherwise indicated, quoted material in this and the following chapter is from Father McGuckin's correspondence.

[2] Sister Edith Downs, *A Century of Service*, Victoria, p. 61.

[3] Correspondence of Bishop Louis D'herbomez to Sister Mary Providence, Summer 1865, A.S.S.A. Victoria.

[4] Father McGuckin is referring to Section II, paragraph C of the "Ordinance to establish a uniform system of Public Education throughout the Province," passed in the Legislature, February 24, 1869.

[5] Minutes of the Council Meeting of the Vicariate of British Columbia, January 9, 1871, Oblate History, U.B.C.

[6] Durieu to Mother Mary Eulalie, December 1, 1873, A.S.S.A. Lachine.

[7] D'herbomez to Mother Mary Eulalie, February 22, 1873, A.S.S.A. Lachine.

[8] Besson, *Un Missionaire d'Autrefois*, p. 23.

[9] Durieu to Mother Mary Eulalie, December 1, 1873, A.S.S.A. Lachine.

[10] Minutes of the Council Meeting of the Sisters of St. Ann, Lachine, December 27, 1873, A.S.S.A. Lachine.

[11] Donald Maclaurin, "The History of Education in the Crown Colonies of Vancouver Island and British Columbia and in the Colony of British Columbia," Doctoral Thesis, University of Washington, 1936, p. 48.

[12] Deliberations du Conseil Provincial, February 23, 1876, A.D.

[13] "Notes from Lachine," Manuscript, A.S.S.A. Victoria.

[14] Sister Marie Infant Jesus to Reverend Mother Irene, Lachine, July 12, 1930, A.S.S.A. Victoria.

[15] *Ibid.*

Chapter VI

"TOO MANY IRONS IN THE FIRE"

The missionary work at St. Joseph's which had started out with such promise was suffering from neglect. The ranch and the schools were absorbing more and more personnel, and the important promise that Father McGuckin made to the Cariboo Indian chiefs to educate their children remained unfulfilled. It was not until 1877 that Father McGuckin began to campaign in earnest for Indian education and then his reasons had little to do with Indian literacy:

> In a few years hence, all our young boys and girls will speak English, mix with the whites and lose all of their original simplicity. To resist then the temptations that will be placed in their way nothing less than a thorough religious education will suffice. This they will never acquire in their own language. Not as children, for during childhood there is no opportunity so long as they remain with their parents. Not during boyhood or girlhood, for then they are too busy and can only be formed for a short time in the Winter, and often then unwilling to occupy their spare time at religious instruction. We must endeavour to get them in to School and keep them for a certain number of years.

When in reply the Bishop suggested opening day schools for the Indian children of Cariboo, Stuart Lake, and Kamloops, Father McGuckin instantly demurred. Although he was "quite willing" to open the day schools for Indian boys, unless the Bishop was able to provide new school buildings and, more importantly, "good competent teachers" day schools would fail.

In the spring of 1880, Father McGuckin heard that Bishop D'herbomez was opening a school for white girls at Kamloops under the direction of the Sisters of St. Ann. Presuming that the Bishop would, "as soon as possible," open a second school for boys, the Irish Oblate formulated a plan to answer the question of Indian education in the Cariboo. This plan — or rather a "reflection on School Affairs in the Interior" as Father McGuckin referred to it — he lay before the Bishop. He began his rather lengthy but meticulously detailed exposition by reminding D'herbomez that in the four mission districts in the Interior the Indian children were without a single school. The children under the guidance of Our Lady of Good Hope Mission, Stuart Lake, were deemed "safe enough" for the moment as they were receiving considerable instruction in their religious duties from Father LeJacq. By contrast the children of the Cariboo, Okanagan, and Kamloops region were "as a general rule" growing up without religious instruction and consequently without receiving the sacraments. The missionaries were insisting on young men and women learning some catechism and going to confession before marriage but many of the young men never returned for further instruction after marriage. Continuing to press his case, the Oblate warned that the Indians who had grown up lacking religious instruction were "advancing rapidly every day in the pride, indifference, and vices of their heretical and infidel neighbours." Returning here to a now familiar theme, Father McGuckin reminded the Bishop that the Oblates in the Cariboo had so far been "little troubled with heretical Ministers — but let them come?" he added ominously.

To remedy the situation, Father McGuckin suggested that the proposed schools at Kamloops take all the white and Métis children of the Cariboo, Kamloops, Yale, Lytton, and Lillooet districts. And, since railway and steamboat transportation would render Kamloops "a convenient place" for pupils from Victoria, they should be accommodated also. The schools at St. Joseph's could then be given over entirely to Indian education. The Mission had resources which, if supplemented by a government grant and managed well, could support one hundred Indian children "judiciously chosen from the various Indian villages." The Oblate was convinced that "with God's help" the children, when "thoroughly instructed and trained in their necessary duties," would be the means of restoring the Indians of the Cariboo to the Catholic Church. If something more was not done to instruct the young people, "twenty years hence" the Mission would have lost all.

Father McGuckin was not exaggerating the danger to Oblate work in the Cariboo. In June 1873, Bishop D'herbomez unwittingly dealt the first blow to successful Indian work when he transferred Father LeJacq to Stuart Lake. The devoted Durieu disciple and dedicated Indian missionary went north to open a mission for the Northern Carrier peoples; with him went Brother Blanchet who, in order that there might be two priests at the new mission, agreed

Cariboo Shuswap Warrior.

The first church built at St. Joseph's Mission, circa 1900.

Founder Bishop Charles Joseph Eugene de Mazenod.

UNLESS OTHERWISE NOTED ALL PHOTOS ARE COLLECTION OF THE AUTHOR.

1st Bishop, Cariboo Mission, Louis D'herbomez.

2nd Bishop, Cariboo Mission, Paul Durieu.

Sisters of the Child Jesus at the Cariboo Mission: left to right, Sister Eloide, Sister Assumption, Sister Fabian, Sister Octavia, Sister Euphrasia, Sister Seraphim, Sister Alix, circa 1910.

Sisters of the Child Jesus, lay teachers and children in front of the girls' school and convent, at St. Joseph's Mission, circa 1900.

Men and boys at the Cariboo Mission at the endless job of chopping and stacking wood for fuel, circa 1900.

PHOTO COURTESY: MRS. JOSEPHINE BOB

Sisters of the Child Jesus picking raspberries at the Mission, August 26, 1908.

PHOTO COURTESY: MRS. JOSEPHINE BOB

The Mission: Taken around 1910, this photograph shows the priests' and boys' residence, the original log church and the sisters' and girls' convent. In the foreground is the Mission cemetery; apart from two or three farm buildings, this is all that remains of the original Mission.

Father Jean-Marie LeJacq.

Father James Marie McGuckin.

Father Charles Marchal.

Sister Marie Clement, S.S.A.

Sister Marie Octavie, S.S.A.

Sister Marie Joachim, S.S.A.

The first Sisters of St. Ann for the Cariboo Mission.

First Indian Sister: Sister Henrietta from Deep Creek was the Cariboo's — and the province's — first Indian nun. She is seen here with her family, circa 1911.

PHOTO COURTESY: MRS. JOSEPHINE BOB

Sister Henrietta and her father. Photograph taken between 1911 and 1918.

PHOTO COURTESY: MRS. JOSEPHINE BOB

Father François Marie Thomas with two Indian postulants at Anaham reserve, 1947.

Father Thomas outside his home on an Indian reserve in the Cariboo.

Built in 1885, the priests' and boys' residence was up-graded by a grant from the federal government in 1894. The wooden buildings were destroyed by fire in 1954.

Class of 1908-1909 at St. Joseph's Mission. In the front row, far left, is Celestine Johnson.

PHOTO COURTESY: MRS. JOSEPHINE BOB

Washday at the Mission: a Sister of the Child Jesus supervises the older girls as they do the weekly wash.

PHOTO COURTESY: MRS. JOSEPHINE BOB

The weekly wash finished and hanging on the line, four girls from St. Joseph's Mission pose in their finery.

PHOTO COURTESY: MRS. JOSEPHINE BOB

Bishop Dontenwill (centre), flanked by Father Casimir Chirouse and Father Jean Marie LeJeune, celebrate the completion and blessing of St. Paul's Canoe Creek Church, in 1902.

Part of the crowd gathered to celebrate the blessing of the Canoe Creek Church.

Canoe Creek Indians and friends celebrating the blessing of their new church, 1902.

Remains of the original church, St. Gabriel's, built at Canoe Creek in 1868.

PHOTO: JOHN BRIOUX

to be ordained at this time. The previous April, Father LeJacq had willingly relinquished his role as Superior of the Mission to Father McGuckin; LeJacq was an "in-the-field" missionary, preferring his months among the Indians to the restraint of desk work. Now, having gained Indian acceptance of Durieu's method in the Cariboo, he was sent to begin again further north. The Bishop sent Father Marchal as Father LeJacq's replacement. Although he had had experience of missionary work among the Sechelts and the Indians of the Lower Fraser at St. Mary's Mission, where the Durieu method was being implemented, Father Marchal did not have the same charismatic appeal for the Indians as Father LeJacq. He could not rouse the response which the Indians had accorded his predessor.

The importance of a missionary's personal appeal for the Indians could not have been more clearly revealed than in the developments between Father Marchal and the Shuswap and Lower Carriers of Soda Creek, Alexandria, and Quesnel. Father Marchal tried valiantly to reach and instruct all these Indian bands, as well as the widespread and distant Chilcotin. Often he would be back at the Mission only a short time before leaving again to visit other camps. During November and December 1874, for example, travelling either by canoe or on foot, Father Marchal travelled west to visit several camps of Chilcotin, then circled round to visit the Shuswap of Canoe Creek and Alkali Lake. He went on to Soda Creek to administer the sacraments to elderly Indians who were unable to travel to the Mission. He returned to St. Joseph's for the Christmas celebrations with the local Shuswap, then left once more on January 2, 1875. This time he travelled north to the Indians of Alexandria and Quesnel. On this journey he was expected to pay a visit to the white Catholics of St. Patrick's parish but, because he had to travel south to visit the Indians of Lillooet and the surrounding district and return to the Mission for Easter celebrations he was obliged to put off this visit until April. In spite of his efforts, Father Marchal began to lose ground with the Indians.

As early as 1875, there were indications that Father Marchal was having difficulties. Father McGuckin wrote to the Bishop requesting another priest for St. Joseph's, "one who will gain the good will of the Indians." The matter was urgent since the Indians were becoming "dissatisfied" with Father Marchal and, consequently, many were becoming "indifferent" towards the Catholic religion. By the following January, Father Marchal had visibly lost the regard of several Shuswap bands. In 1875, he had given Chief

William, Chief of the former Chimney Creek Indians now camped at the Mission, permission to allow the young men of the camp to sing one of their traditional Indian songs. That the Chief had asked permission indicated not a rejection of Christianity but rather a desire to combine the old and the new. Unfortunately for Father Marchal, he lacked the insight of one of his successors, Father Adrian Morice, who, with regard to giving rules to the Indians, observed that:

> Once given that decision cannot be repealed, once out, that order must ever stand good under pain of suggesting either indecision, therefore weakness or even ignorance, which, in a superior would do away with all respect on the part of the inferior. A man who can make a mistake has no right to command according to the Indians.[1]

Father Marchal was to suffer the consequences of his liberalism. The permission was given for one occasion only but the Indians continued to revive the old songs in defiance of the priest. Consequently, Indians at Canoe Creek, Dog Creek, and Alkali Lake returned also to singing "bad songs" and, defiantly, they revived Indian dancing and gambling games. When the Indian bands gathered at the Mission for Christmas and New Year's celebrations, Father Marchal tried to persuade the Indians to give up their singing and other "bad habits" to which they had returned but both Chief William and the Chief of Soda Creek refused to give up the singing. The Indians' refusal to reject their ancient customs, an absolute necessity under Durieu's system for reception of the sacraments, put the missionaries under the necessity of refusing to accept their confessions as sincere, and the Indians were refused absolution; a stand-off situation arose. Fully occupied himself in his administrative role, Father McGuckin lamented the lack of a priest who would gain the Indians' respect and reverse the "backsliding."

In 1876, Chief William had what Father McGuckin described as "a severe attack of sickness" and, as he began to fear that death was imminent, he gave up his "singing mania" and returned to the Church. Consequently all the Williams Lake band went to confession at Easter. The Soda Creek Chief however remained "in revolt" against the Mission and most of his Indians followed his example. The breach between Father Marchal and some of the Indians continued to widen. During the 1877 Christmas celebrations, when in spite of the unsettled situation a good many of the unrepentant Indians arrived at St. Joseph's, Father Marchal attempted once more to instruct them; yet his efforts were unsuccessful. He even preached in Shuswap deviating from the Durieu plan which insisted on the use of interpreters. But, in spite of Father Marchal's conviction that he pronounced the language well, the Indians disparaged his pronunciation. Father Marchal was distressed but "all his efforts for them were of no use."

As the Mission Superior, Father McGuckin enumerated for the Bishop the shortcomings of every priest and Brother sent to St. Joseph's — and in this respect Father Marchal was no exception. Although the most persistent critic, Father McGuckin however was not the only Oblate to remark on Father Marchal's difficulties. According to Father LeJacq, Father Marchal "vainly rebuked, chided and reproached, he was preaching in the desert."[2] In his *Memoirs*, Father Thomas came to the same conclusion and indicated that Father Marchal's problems were personality related. "Father Marchal threatened and thundered in vain," he wrote, "Father LeJacq alone had sufficient influence to keep the Shuswaps on the straight and narrow path or to bring them back when they fell into their old disorders."

The "revolt" spread and in the summer of 1879 the Indians at Kluskus Lake refused to give up their feasts and the Indians at Fort Alexandria were also returning to their old patterns. The Indians closest to the Mission began to show "great want of fervour" and among some bands "all the savage practices, chants, dances, feasts which they had given up in order to embrace Christianity were reinstated in force."[3] But it was not Father Marchal alone who was causing the problem, for, despite his apparent lack of rapport with the Indians, no other missionary was assigned to replace him or assist him. Here lay the crux of the problem, a lack of missionary manpower to capitalize on the Indians' interest in Christianity. As early as August 1874 Father McGuckin wrote to the Bishop with a warning that lack of manpower was a serious impediment to Indian missionary work:

> It is impossible for us to manage the school and give fair play to the Indians. We must have time to study the Indian language or our Mission is bound to fall behind. We cannot get interpreters half the time we want them, and besides the children and young boys and girls are much neglected because we cannot give them the instruction which they need to preserve them from evil and teach them to lead Christian lives. What a pity it is to see people so well disposed, so much neglected!

By 1878 the Chilcotins, "owing to their wandering life and difficulty of being able to communicate with them" — a difficulty compounded by the unpredictable Chilcotin response to arranged meetings — had not been visited for almost two years and apparently knew more about the Catholic faith "five years ago" than they did at present. The missionaries were aware that in order for missionary work among the Chilcotin to be successful, a priest needed to first learn the language and then reside a few months a year among them when they were encamped. However, James McGuckin warned the Bishop, "when there are too many irons in the fire, some of them must grow cold."

The Irish Oblate was ever ready to pinpoint the difficulties of converting and encouraging so many diverse and widespread peoples, but he himself was part of the problem. He was a dedicated Oblate, but he was not by nature a dedicated Indian missionary. Eugene de Mazenod would have been proud of Father McGuckin, whom he had met during the Irish Oblate's stay in Marseilles. James McGuckin was determined to observe the rules of the founder to the letter; and, regardless of circumstances, those who came under his direction were expected to be equally scrupulous. In the spring of 1869 the Bishop and his Council appointed Father McGuckin as "Admonitor," a position for which he was eminently suited. It was his task to safeguard "the bodily and spiritual welfare" of the Mission Superior. This meant that he had to watch over Father LeJacq's health, attending to all necessary expenses for his food, clothing, and other temporal wants. In addition, he had to admonish Father LeJacq on any disregard of the *Constitutions and Rules*. Unfortunately for Father McGuckin, Father LeJacq was more concerned with his missionary work than he was with the "letter of the law." It was not long before complaints poured into the Bishop of the Indian missionary's disregard for "order, regularity and observance of the rule." Poor Father LeJacq was chided even for neglecting to wash the altar linen he had used at the Mission before setting out to visit the Indians! Until his departure for Stuart Lake, Father LeJacq continued to be a cause of despair for Father McGuckin. When, in 1871, Charles Grandidier was appointed the Spiritual Prefect of the lay Brothers — whose job it was to see that the lay Brothers observed the rule "very exactly" — and spent a few months at the Mission, Father McGuckin was delighted; he pledged himself to help the "Reverend Father Prefect" all he could in establishing observance of the rule.

When informed by Bishop D'herbomez that he was to be Superior at St. Joseph's, the Irish Oblate was pleased to accept the new role as he had been "anxious . . . to see our Holy Rule observed at this Mission." He requested immediately the replacement of a lay Brother with one who was "a good Religious." In spite of the shortage of "in-the-field" missionaries, over the next ten years, Father McGuckin insisted on rigid adherence to the rules. A missionary returning from a circuit of several weeks or several months was nonetheless expected to participate in retreats and conferences. In February 1873, Father LeJacq, returning after a long missionary tour and preparing to leave St. Joseph's for his new obedience at Stuart Lake, had to participate in Conferences on the Sacraments of Baptism, Matrimony, and Penance. Reporting to the Bishop on the outcome of the conference, Father McGuckin wrote that after the conference "a Retreat was commenced . . . everything being done according to our Ceremonial."

After the departure of Father LeJacq and until the establishment of the school and the consequent arrival of a number of priests, Father Marchal had to bear the brunt of Father McGuckin's obsession with the rules. The strain of continuous travel and the increasing problems with the Indians would have sufficed to make even a patient man somewhat irritable at times — and Charles Marchal was far from being a patient man. In the brief periods he spent at the Mission he preferred to relax by doing carpentry, a natural, and one would think, a useful occupation for the Mission. But Father McGuckin, concerned over Father Marchal's "lack of perseverance" in observing the rules, desired him when at the Mission to remain in his room and follow the regular exercises of the Community "for months at a time." Pressure of work was no excuse for a poor religious life, and the Irish Oblate reported to the Bishop "the fact of trying to have our Holy Rules strictly observed, urges me on to practise what I preach." While Father de Mazenod may have considered him an exemplary Oblate, his fellow workers no doubt wished that Father McGuckin was a more practical Indian missionary.

Father McGuckin was in fact far happier behind a desk than travelling for months on end to preach to the Indians. In 1870, he did offer to open a new mission at Stuart Lake but, as his letters reveal, he was quite certain that the area was destined to become a prosperous and populous one. He noted that quite a number of ranches were being pre-empted in the area and that the prospects of new mines there would attract "a great rush" from California.

From time to time the Irish Oblate visited one or two Indian bands but once the school was flourishing he left most of the missionary work to Father Marchal. When in December 1876 Paul Durieu paid a visit to the Mission, he insisted that Father McGuckin take up his share of missionary activity and visit the local Indians and all those north of the Mission on a regular basis. The Irish Oblate protested to Bishop D'herbomez that he was far too preoccupied with the schools, and would not be able to undertake such a visit until the next school vacation.

The development of the white schools were in fact another reason for the neglect of the Indians. In December 1877, Father McGuckin complained to the Bishop that while the pupils were progressing well, it was "not quite so well" as he wished. In a most revealing statement he wrote:

> I have so many occupations that it is impossible for me to spend long enough with them.... Next Wednesday I intend to leave to visit the Indians of Soda Creek and Quesnelle [sic] and will be absent about 18 days. This upsets everything and often I am disturbed during my classes, hence the school suffers.

Father McGuckin made it plain that he could not leave the school to visit the Indians "even for a week or two at a time," in spite of the fact that it was "utterly useless" for Father Marchal to do so. In his *Memoirs* Father Thomas pointed out that because so many priests were required to teach in the school, the overburdened Indian missionary had to add more Indian bands "to his flock."

In 1880, Father Marchal moved to Stuart Lake and the Oblates who taught in the school visited the Indians whenever they could. Father Guertin, who had been sent to the school in 1879, had not been happy as a teacher and, for a while, he interested himself in the Indians, "liking very well to ride around and visit the Indian villages, studying their languages and attempting to write out the Chilcotin language." These visits, while maintaining the contact, did little to advance the Indians' commitment to Catholicism. "Whether through the fault of the Fathers, Indians or circumstances" the Indians were receiving no serious instruction. "It both pains and grieves me," wrote Father McGuckin, "to see many of our Indians who have seriously violated the first promises made 13 years ago, and yet not one of them is sufficiently instructed to receive Holy Communion." When Father Morice arrived at St. Joseph's in 1882, he concurred with Father McGuckin's conclusions regarding the spiritual neglect of the Indians. Commenting particularly on the neglect of the Chilcotin, Father Morice wrote that despite previous visits by the missionaries, they were ignorant of the truths of the Catholic faith. He caused "une véritable tempête" among the Indians when he refused to baptize a number of Chilcotins because of their lack of knowledge. Father Morice wrote to a friend that the Chilcotin informed him that missionaries postponed baptizing them year after year and, in the end, they had not returned,[4] a sad comment on what had been a promising missionary situation.

However, if the spiritual well-being of the Indians was neglected, the Mission did take an interest in their material well-being, for although Father McGuckin did not always place the interests of the Indians first, he, like other missionaries, recognized the need to help the Indian in his dealings with white law. The first recorded instance of Father McGuckin's concern in this area arose in February 1873 when Charles Marchal, acting under the orders of Father Durieu, began to make changes in the manner of recording births, marriages, and deaths. Father McGuckin felt that with regards to marriages the new format was illegal and that the children of wrongly recorded marriages would not be able "to prove the rights of their legitimacy before the Civil Courts." Although at present this might not be of much consequence, the priest thought that futuristically, with some Indians already beginning to acquire property, "it may be of considerable importance."

While in Victoria later that year, Father McGuckin visited the Federal Indian Superintendent, Dr. Israel Wood Powell, to discover his attitude towards the Indian reserve problem. "He told me," the priest wrote to the Bishop, "that there was a difficulty between the Federal and Provincial Governments about the quantity of land to be given to each Indian family. The former are not willing to give as much as the latter demands." The Oblate solicited a promise from Dr. Powell that he would send to the Mission any medicine required by the Indians. This was a concern of the Oblate Superior because, unless the government provided help, the Mission would have to continue providing free medication. In the summer of 1874, Marcus Smith, a Canadian government surveyor, visited the Mission. Smith was in the area supervising surveying parties searching for a possible railway route to the coast via the Cariboo. However, he had a secondary objective. He told Father McGuckin that he had been commissioned by the Canadian government to use the opportunity to obtain information about the British Columbia Indians. According to the Oblate, Smith appeared to be "very desirous" of obtaining justice for the Indians and intended using what influence he had with the government in Ottawa "to obtain for them such assistance and grants of land as they stand in need of." Mr. Smith appeared to have a good opinion of Dr. Powell and Mr. Lenihan, but remarked that the latter had "no idea of Indian Affairs" — not surprising given that prior to his appointment as Indian Superintendent, James Lenihan was a Toronto businessman totally unfamiliar with the Indians.[5] The Oblate obtained a promise from Smith that he would do "all in his power" for the Indians of the Mission.

In July 1874, Bishop D'herbomez sent a petition to St. Joseph's and requested Father McGuckin to see that it was signed by the Indian Chiefs of the Cariboo. The petition was a request for a fair deal for the Indians in regard to land allocation, and the Bishop intended to send copies of the signed document to the "Council of Indian Affairs" in Victoria, to the Federal Government and, if necessary, "to the Queen in England." In an accompanying letter, the Bishop exhorted his missionaries to defend the interests of the Indians and assist them in obtaining the land they were claiming for themselves and their children; they were to encourage the people to be "firm and energetic" in pressing their just claims and caution them to resist any call to war.[6] In spite of the Bishop's request, Father McGuckin was reluctant to circulate the petition. A month earlier he had met Doctor Powell "on the road to Boston Bar," and the Indian Superintendent had promised some of the Cariboo bands that either he or James Lenihan would visit the Cariboo during July; the priest felt that it would be best to wait and see what the government proposed. After this meeting, the Indians would be better acquainted with government policy and would know "what they want and what they should ask for."

As Father McGuckin anticipated, the Indians were not interested in signing the petition until they had seen the Indian Commissioner and knew what he proposed to do for them. "They want to talk to him themselves," wrote the priest, "before making any complaint or demand." Apparently while they were prepared to be guided spiritually by the missionaries, the Indians were not yet prepared to be advised by them in material matters. The question of reserve land had become pressing, especially in regard to the Cariboo Shuswap. The Indians of the Williams Lake area, Canoe Creek, and others had already been displaced by the pre-emptions of white ranchers. Although they realized that they needed to lay claim to some areas as soon as possible, there was "not even 40 acres" left that was fit for cultivation. Unless the government was willing to purchase land from the white settlers, there was not even forty acres of farming land for each Indian family between Lillooet and Cariboo — unless the government was prepared to go to great expense and irrigate large areas. If Doctor Powell did not keep his promise to visit the Indians, Father McGuckin felt sure that, under such distressing circumstances, there would be no further difficulty in bringing the Indians to see the wisdom of signing the petition.

Three years passed without much being resolved and the priest even had difficulty obtaining from the government the implements and medicines he had requested for the Indians. In August 1877, exasperated by government procrastination, James McGuckin began his own campaign to pressure Lenihan into settling land claims for the Cariboo Indians. "It is certain the Indians have been badly used," he wrote to Lenihan, "and they have been tampered with by settlers and nothing less than a speedy settlement will restore peace in their minds."[7] In response, two months later James Lenihan paid a four-day visit to the Mission. He saw Chief William at St. Joseph's and promised to send farming implements to Williams Lake; he promised the priest he would send them also to Soda Creek and the Chilcotin Indians. He looked at the Indian land situation, "but of course" wrote Father McGuckin "he could do nothing." In early spring, Father McGuckin informed the Commissioner that during his recent visits to the Indians of Quesnel, Alexandria, Soda Creek, and Williams Lake, the people "repeatedly expressed their anxiety about the settlement of their land question." The Indians of Soda Creek were particularly concerned as quartz had been discovered near their land and they feared another invasion of miners into their territory. The Oblate warned that the Indians were becoming agitated;[8] two months later he wrote again in stronger terms:

> The Indians in this section are becoming very discontented and using threatening language on account of the delay in settling their reserves. I have used all my endeavours to keep them quiet up to the present but it is evident that they will not heed me much longer in this matter if something is not done for them immediately.[9]

In spite of these warnings, another eighteen months passed by without any change in the situation, until in November, the point of desparation was reached as many Indians of the Cariboo faced starvation after a bad salmon run and a poor hunting season.

A letter written by Chief William was published in the *Daily British Colonist*. Father McGuckin claimed to his Bishop that he had no part in writing the letter, but Mr. Kelly, who wrote what the Chief dictated, was employed as a teacher at the Mission. The letter told of the starvation of Chief William's people. Since all the land and the fish had been taken by the white man, and "the noise of the threshing machine and wagon" had frightened the game and the beaver, the Indians had nothing to eat. Consequently the young men were threatening to ignore the Chief and go to war. Four days after the letter appeared in the press, Lenihan wrote to Father McGuckin stating he "disbelieved the whole or most of it." The missionary however corroborated Chief William's statement. He wrote to Lenihan that he was already assisting the Indians to keep them from starving, that the Indians did not have land enough to raise one-tenth of the crops they required for their support, and that the young men would have "recourse to violence" rather than die of starvation. "In addition," wrote Father McGuckin, "the Chief of the Alkali Lake tribe told Father Marchal that his young men were urging him to allow them to go to war with the whites. The Chilcotin and many other I know will only be too glad to join them in order to have the opportunity of avenging old wrongs." The only way of pacifying them, warned the priest, was for the government "to afford immediate relief to those in want" and to assure the Indians that there would be no further delay in settling their claims.[10] As a result of this letter, Lenihan sent a telegram to Vankoughnet in Ottawa: "Father McGuckin collaborates statement condition Indians in Williams Lake district, would recommend immediate relief." The relief arrived in the form of flour and meat — although Vankoughnet recommended that the Indians be made to work for the relief sent.

In his *Memoirs* Father Thomas told the story of how Father McGuckin assisted the Indians living across the San José from the Mission. The winter of 1879 was severe and the snow "unbelievably deep." While hunting, "the father of Baptiste kra-al" got his snow-shoes caught in the branches of a snow-covered fir tree and hung there for approximately two hours until discovered by another hunter. Apparently Father McGuckin and the local Indian Agent James McKinley "profited by the accident" to pressure the government to review the case of the landless Indians. As a result, the government bought Mr. Bates' ranch near Williams Lake and some land at Deep Creek for this band. The band moved from the Mission, "leaving behind a small cemetery near the present P.G.E. station where the Indians buried a small girl who was drowned on her way to the Mission," and settled at what is now the Sugar Cane reserve. (According to Father Thomas, it is named Sugar Cane because the tall grass which grows there is much relished by horses; the Indian name was "Plulchorshishin," which was the name given to a small red-mouthed fish which used to swim up Borland Creek.)

Although the land question was of primary importance to the Indians, a second problem was developing; this was the availability of liquor to many of the bands. In July 1874, Bishop D'herbomez sent a "Prohibition Petition" to St. Joseph's and told his missionaries to obtain the signatures of both Indians and whites. The "Methodist or Presbyterian Society of Ontario" was circulating the petition which was to be presented at the next Dominion Parliament Session. As might be expected, Father McGuckin was opposed to the petition on the grounds that it was circulated by Protestants. Rather than follow the lead of Methodists and Presbyterians, he suggested that the Bishop send out a purely Catholic petition. With regards to obtaining signatures, the Irish Oblate expected problems with the Cariboo's white population. A law recently passed restricting the brewing of liquor to Victoria and New Westminster had upset local farmers because it lessened the opportunity of selling their grain. It had also angered saloon-keepers, brewers, and "beer-drinkers in general," causing a "growl" which the priest thought made it an inappropriate time to ask for signatures. Father McGuckin did not expect any resistance from the Indians whom he confidently expected to willingly sign.

Since drunkenness was considered a serious sin — and this was especially stressed by Paul Durieu — those Indians who wished to receive the sacraments had to resist the temptation of liquor. The missionary's law was fully supported by the Chiefs who, as time went by, became greatly alarmed by the availability and consequences of alcohol. The Indian Chiefs, particularly those of Quesnel, Alexandria, Soda Creek, and the Williams Lake area where their people were in regular contact with the whites, were concerned because the authorities in the district "were not willing to go to any trouble to suppress the liquor traffic." It was illegal to sell drink to the Indians yet people who were bootlegging were going unpunished "through the neglect of the authorities." The Chiefs were concerned about their people and wished to have "some means of punishing evil doers." They asked Father McGuckin to write to the government authorities for them. "They wished to know," wrote the Oblate to Lenihan, "how much the government will contribute towards the erection of suitable lock-ups" as he felt that the Indians present mode of punishment — which he does not specify — was "too rigorous."

Father McGuckin also resisted bootleggers in a more direct manner. According to Lawrence Guichon, a well-known pioneer rancher, Father McGuckin would patrol the Sugar Cane reserve during the evening watching for bootleggers. One evening, he met a man going to the reserve with several bottles of liquor. When Father McGuckin, who knew the man, tried to prevent him entering the reserve the man became angry and abusive. He dared the missionary to stop him; "you depend on that black robe to protect you," he taunted. "Not so much as I do on this good right arm," answered Father McGuckin, and "forthwith proceeded to prove it."[11] As a spokesman for the Indians during these years of change, Father McGuckin helped to maintain a good rapport between them and the Church, as missionary spiritual endeavours continued to be neglected.

NOTES TO CHAPTER VI

1 Father Adrian Morice, *Fifty Years in Western Canada*, Toronto, 1930, p. 48.

2 Father LeJacq to the Superior General, October 25, 1895, Manuscript, O.A.

3 *Ibid.*

4 *Missions*, 1883, p. 357.

5 On the unsuitability of Lenihan and other government appointees, Fisher, *Contact and Conflict*, Chapter 7.

6 Bishop D'herbomez to Father McGuckin, July 16, 1874; Bishop D'herbomez to Father Julian Baudre, April 15, 1874. Dossier D'herbomez, File No. G-LPP, 1435, Folio 15, 16, A.G. Rome.

7 Father McGuckin to Lenihan, August 23, 1877, Miscellaneous Box 17, Legislative Library, Victoria.

8 Father McGuckin to Lenihan, February 14, 1878, Microfilm B-292, C10119, P.A.B.C.

9 *Ibid.*, April 10, 1878.

10 *Ibid.*, November 22, 1879.

11 Cronin, *Cross in the Wilderness*, p. 118.

Chapter VII

"THE GOLDEN AGE"

Until 1890, notwithstanding individual missionary efforts to revive and strengthen the faith of the Cariboo's Indians, the *status quo* remained unchanged. Then, in May 1890, in a move that was to have fortunate repercussions for the work of the Cariboo's missionaries, Paul Durieu and the Sechelt chiefs planned a gathering of Indian tribes at the Sechelt village. Its purpose was to mark the dedication of a new church which the Sechelt people had just completed. Invitations were dispatched to the various Indian tribes under the care of Oblate missionaries. Father Jean-Marie Le Jeune, missionary at Kamloops, obtained special rates from railway officials for Indians attending the gathering and Father Marchal, who had returned to the Mission in 1887 after an eight-year absence, took a group of Shuswap and Carrier Indians to participate in the event. As Father LeJacq later recorded, the visit was greatly beneficial to St. Joseph's missionary endeavours.

It has been said that Paul Durieu "understood" the Indians. To what extent he did so is open to conjecture, but certainly the elaborate community-orientated ceremonials attached to the solemn opening of new churches helped to fulfil the Indians' need "to celebrate religious and mystical aspects of existence."[1] This was a time when both government officials and missionaries were attempting to suppress the Indian ceremonial known as the Potlatch and the Indians were being forced to go underground to continue their traditional celebrations. In Church ceremonials, such as the blessing of a new church, the Indians could find a Christian and legally acceptable substitute for the Potlatch. This is not to suggest that a Church ceremony could totally replace an ancient Indian rite. But the Indians had a highly developed appreciation of symbolism, mysticism, and solemnity, and Catholic ceremonials were steeped in centuries-old traditions, highly symbolic of past history. In addition there were very visible synchronizations. As with the Potlatch, during the week of the consecration of the church, all work was put aside; one Indian band played host to many others; the wealth of the host group could be displayed in the costly exterior and interior of the church; ritual dances were replaced by religious ceremonials, with all Indians participating; the host village fed and entertained its visitors, and the way was opened for visiting groups to reciprocate.

The Sechelt village was considered a model for other Indian bands. It was constructed along the lines of a white village or small town, with symmetrical rows of neat houses. The new twin-towered church dominated the village. In May, delegations from a dozen or more tribes arrived for the ceremonials, each group accompanied by its local missionary. Seven chapels were prepared on the outskirts of the village where the Indians could, through the use of interpreters, hear preaching in their own language. Paul Durieu and Bishop John Nicholas Lemmens of Vancouver Island headed the twenty-two Oblate priests present at the gathering. Durieu commenced the celebrations with the blessing of the new church in the presence of almost two thousand Indians. As usual the ceremonies were elaborate and impressive. Thirty Indians were selected as a guard of honour for the Eucharist which was exposed in the new church, and there were two solemn processions in which Indian children strewed flowers and the adults carried statues and candles in a picture reminiscent of European religious processions.[2]

This event was impressive in itself, but the gathering was interrupted by the death of Bishop D'herbomez. Bishop Durieu hurried back to New Westminster accompanied by all the Indian chiefs and principal men of each band at the gathering, including those from the Cariboo. All officiated in the solemn ceremonies marking the Bishop's funeral — a second impressive demonstration. On their return home, the Cariboo Indians "related the wonders of which they had been spectators and excited lively regrets in the hearts of their compatriots"; in the words of Father LeJacq, "there came a revolution in spirits." In October, the Shuswap band of Alkali Lake held a festival similar to the one some of their people had seen at Sechelt; again, the reason was the blessing of a new church. All the Indian bands of St. Joseph's Mission district were invited and Bishop Durieu, accompanied by Father LeJacq whom Durieu had re-posted to the Mission, Father Chirouse, and Father LeJeune, presided at the event. After this celebration the Indians of Sugar Cane

Reserve resolved, "in a general assembly of the whole village" — a total of approximately 150 people — to replace their old church with a new one, and hold a like festival at its completion; a religious revival was underway in the Cariboo.

The gathering of the bands at Sugar Cane from July 9th to July 15th, 1895, indicated that the influence of Paul Durieu was clearly at work once more in the Cariboo.[3] In preparation for the visit by the Bishop, the Indians prepared an area of land large enough to accommodate all the bands who arrived. They built an "arch of triumph," hung it with Venetian and Chinese lanterns, and placed a throne beneath the arch for the Bishop. They then organized a place of honour for each visiting chief and his band. At the beginning of the festivities a group of "élite" young men from each tribe was chosen to ride ahead of the Bishop's carriage from the Mission house to the reserve. A volley of rifles was fired as Bishop Durieu reached Sugar Cane and, after he was seated ceremoniously on the throne and greeted by the chiefs, an Indian read a welcoming speech. Hymns and solemn benediction followed.

During the following six days the Indians followed strict procedures. A bell awoke everyone at 5:00 a.m. Morning prayers began at six and were followed by a few minutes of silent contemplation, a hymn, and Mass. After breakfast a "grand session" was held. In these sessions several matters were attended to: "abuses" were corrected; "delinquents" were censured; differences between individual Indians were "terminated"; the catechism was explained, and the Indians practised new hymns. In the late afternoon, prayers and hymns were followed by benediction and a second "grand session." To ensure that everyone attended the services — for the weather was tropically hot and the cool water of Williams Lake was very tempting — Bishop Durieu posted watchmen equipped with notebooks and pencils to watch for those who succumbed to temptation. In the evening a list of all these "delinquents" was tacked on Bishop Durieu's door. All retired at ten o'clock and watchmen were posted to enforce the curfew.

As well as reinforcing the Durieu System among the Indians, the Bishop used the celebrations at Sugar Cane as an opportunity to inaugurate his Indian Total Abstinence Society of British Columbia in St. Joseph's Mission district. The Society, with the Bishop as president, was a "regular association" with a constitution, regulations, and statutes. Consequently it enjoyed all the rights and privileges of a regular association. The Bishop wished to establish a branch of the Society in every Indian village, and the chief — wherever possible the hereditary chief — was made the local president of his branch. As the local president, the chief was empowered "without being subject to arrest and prosecution to maintain order and discipline among the Indian members of the said society." The stress, placed here by Father LeJacq, on the ability of the chief to control his Indians "within the law" resulted from a blow delivered to the Durieu System in 1892 when Father Chirouse Jr. along with a group of Lillooet Indians, including the chief, was arrested and tried by a local magistrate for the whipping of an Indian girl.

The question of whether or not public whipping for offences threatening the common good of the band was part of tribal law before the coming of the missionaries is open to conjecture. Certainly corporal punishment for serious offences was part of nineteenth-century European thinking and at least some missionaries approved its use by Indian chiefs, as witnessed by Father LeJacq's statement:

> Down to recent years, the Chief was enjoying a certain power of repression. He had power to punish severely. The Indian practise gave him the right to lash, handcuff, condemn, to fine, to lock up, to fasting etc. Consequently he was feared and as fear is the beginning of wisdom it meant the reign of order and discipline. Though in the eyes of the government this was an anomoly, still in need of the good resulting, it tolerated it, allowed it to go on, in spite of the frequent reclamations suggested by malevolence and bigotry.

According to Father McGuckin, government did more than tolerate the use of lashing. Writing to Bishop D'herbomez, November 10, 1873, the priest stated that both Judge Begbie and George Walkem, who had become the attorney-general, approved its use. Begbie advised Dr. Foster and the people of Clinton to desist from interfering in the Clinton chief's right to punish his people as he was accustomed to do. Walkem was "most anxious to see the Indian Chiefs use the whip in earnest" and suggested to Father McGuckin that he might try to have a law passed in the coming session of the legislature on the subject.

On March 29, 1892, Father Chirouse, Indian Chief Kilapoutkue of the Lillooets, and two other Indians were charged with inflicting grievous bodily harm on Lucy, a seventeen-year-old Indian girl. Whether through "malevolence and bigotry" or genuine concern for the physical well-being of the Indians, local residents had reported to the magistrate that Lucy had received a severe whipping. Testimony given at the trial proved that the priest was absent when the whipping took place but he had been consulted and suggested the girl receive fifteen lashes for an unspecified sexual offence. After the priest left the village the Chief ordered a further fifteen lashes be administered. The priest and the Indians were found guilty by the local magistrate and given prison sentences. Bishop Durieu appealed to the Governor-General who granted Father Chirouse and the Indians a total remission of the sentence. In light of this event and the publicity it generated, Paul Durieu felt it necessary to establish a totally legal organization within each band — one that would be organized according to white regulations, one that would be encouraged by white society, one that would give the chiefs the same powers as before but closely supervised by the Church. A temperance organization was chosen as the vehicle.

The ten chiefs present at Sugar Cane were instructed to stand near the Bishop at the side of the altar, around which ten temperance flags were draped. The Bishop addressed all the Indians but particularly the chiefs. "You hate drink," he said to them, "but the heart of man is inconsistent especially the heart of the Indian. To aid you to persevere in your good sentiments you are going to be joined together to form a society." Bishop Durieu then explained the constitution and the statutes. According to Father LeJacq, "he indicated the way wherein to exercise control in their villages without leaving themselves open to prosecution in court and without exposing themselves to the pesterings of bad whites." After the Indians had sworn to give up drink, to obey the statutes of the Temperance Society and to submit to the penances given by the chiefs if they failed to keep their pledge, Bishop Durieu presented each chief with a temperance flag. He also promised to send to each village a register containing the Society's statutes, which everyone had to sign. This register was to be deposited at the foot of the altar so that every time the Indians entered the church they would be reminded of their vow to abstain from drink.

Superintending the religious revival and initiating a temperance society were only the first of many changes Paul Durieu instigated at the Mission. In May 1897, he appointed Father Thomas as Indian missionary to St. Joseph's. Father Thomas was born in Brittany in 1868.[4] A typhoid epidemic that killed four of his brothers and sisters left him in poor health, consequently when he first resolved to become a missionary, he met with opposition from his family. His mother and his uncle (a priest who had been appointed

Father Thomas' guardian upon the death of his father) had no objections to the boy becoming a priest but they believed that his health was not good enough for foreign missions. Perseverance in the face of this opposition led François Marie Thomas to the Oblate Novitiate of St. Gerlach in Holland — French law at this time preventing the foundation of an Oblate Novitiate in France — to Liege for his ordination, and finally, in 1894, to Canada. As soon as the young missionary reached New Westminster, Bishop Durieu, in Father Thomas' own words, took him "under his wing." After spending three months on the missions with Father (later Bishop) Bunoz, he was given charge of the Lillooet, Sliammon, Sechelt and Tloos missions. Between visits to these missions, Father Thomas was sent to help various priests or taken to North Vancouver and elsewhere by Bishop Durieu who continued training him for mission work. On one occasion he was put in charge of Holy Rosary parish for a few weeks while Monsignor Emmelen was away and he caused quite a stir by conducting a funeral as it was done in Brittany. Dressed in special garments, including a cope, and accompanied by altar boys and some of the mourners, he went in procession through the streets to the house of the deceased and back to the church. But Father Thomas had no desire to remain a parish priest. He had fought for the opportunity of working among native peoples, and it was with relief that he headed north to take up work at the Mission. Young, energetic, Durieu-trained, and totally devoted to the Bishop and his methods for Indian conversion, Father Thomas was well suited to the task of perpetuating the revival of the Cariboo Indian interest in the Catholic religion. Father Thomas was assigned to attend to the Shuswaps, Carriers, and Chilcotin and while numerically with regard to the Indian work nothing had changed, in François Marie Thomas Bishop Durieu had found a man like himself; for sixty years the missionary followed the Bishop's system faithfully and strictly, and "deviated from certain parts only when this became necessary."[5] And, as they had responded to Father LeJacq, the Cariboo Indians responded well to Father Thomas' efforts for their spiritual welfare.

In the winter of 1899 Father Thomas, walking across the frozen Fraser River, paid his first visit to the Chilcotin bands. He was met on his journey by some Elgatcho Indians who "came a considerable distance" to ask the priest to baptize a young woman who was dying in their village. The Elgatcho were Carrier Indians living north of the Chilcotin country. Father Morice had visited them in

1884 and Father Marchal saw them two years later but these visits had been brief and the priests had taught a few prayers and baptized infants and adults in danger of death but little else. Father Thomas went back with the Elgatcho and not only baptized the Indian girl but spoke to them of the Bishop's plan. He returned to them the following year and organized the village "according to Bishop Durieu's method." He appointed a chief for church affairs, captains and other leaders to preside at the prayers said in public and a watchman "to attend to the good order of the village." During Father Thomas' visit a regular week-long mission was held and attended by Indians from Kluskuz Lake and Ootsa Lake. These visiting Indians proved to be good catechists for they taught the Elgatcho their prayers while Father Thomas "taught the Chief Captains and Watchmen their duties."

A second example of Father Thomas' use of the Durieu System involved the Chilcotin Indians. The passing of the years had not softened the independent attitude of the Chilcotin. In 1880, there was a confrontation between Chilcotin Chief Anaham, a man regarded by Father Thomas as "a man of great intelligence and authority" and a government survey party led by Peter O'Reilly, a man who was appointed Indian Reserve Commissioner even though in the past the Indians had frequently complained about the unfair way he had settled reserves.[6] O'Reilly set the limits of a reserve for Anaham but these did not include the Indians' meadow lands, a particularly fertile and beautiful area. After some discussion, when O'Reilly refused to make the necessary changes, Chief Anaham said to him, "I will give you my last word. No whiteman will ever cut hay in these meadows." O'Reilly, his assistants and policemen returned to their camp to discuss the stalemate. The following morning, deciding that in the case of Anaham it would be wise to acquiesce, O'Reilly sent a messenger asking the Chief to come and resume negotiations. Anaham told the messenger that the commissioner must come to him as Chief Anaham had given his final word the previous evening. Peter O'Reilly returned to the Chief's camp and gave Anaham "the village, its surroundings and the distant meadows." In 1894, Chilcotin Indians staked out a large tract of land in the Chilcotin valley and declared that white men would not be allowed to encroach upon it. When A. G. Vowell, the Indian Superintendent in Victoria, reported the incident to Ottawa, Indian Commissioner Vankoughnet recommended that great prudence be exercised in dealing with the Chilcotin. The Chilcotin had lost none of their spirit.

In 1873, Father McGuckin had understated the situation when he reported that christianizing the Chilcotins would be "a little slow." Father Morice had experienced little success in spite of his efforts for Chilcotin material well-being. According to Norman Lee, well-known Cariboo rancher, Father Morice heard that a white man was planning to pre-empt some Chilcotin land. The priest "got a good horse" and, racing at full speed, reached 150 Mile House in time to pre-empt the land in his own name then turn it over to the Indians. Father Morice blamed the geographical location of the Chilcotin bands for his lack of success, suggesting that the Fraser River created an impossible barrier for much of the year.[7] Father Jean Dominic Chiappini, who had been assigned to work among them after Father Morice left, had tried to convert them for several years without much success. In his opinion, the Chilcotin "had let Redemption pass." Even Father LeJacq could not offer any encouragement to Father Thomas and told him plainly that "he'd never accomplish anything with the Chilcotin." When François Thomas paid his first visit to the Anaham village in 1899, he considered that while among the 275 Chilcotin a good number led excellent lives, the majority still followed the Indian ways. A certain number of the women were living with white men, and Father Thomas saw this as an evil in need of immediate remedy. Evidently the Chilcotin agreed with Father Thomas and the priest spent a week at the village helping to organize the Indians according to Durieu's system. The watchmen and policemen were given the practical task of bringing back to the village "even from great distances" the Chilcotin women living with white men. When necessary they would bring them back a second or third time. According to Father Thomas, in time, these women and their children remained at Anaham and, after the customary year of probation, were baptized. The village of the Anaham band became a regular mission centre for the Chilcotins and Father Thomas was forced to give two, five or six day-long missions at Anaham because so many Indians came.

There was nothing instantaneous about the conversion of the Chilcotin Indians; it was slow painstaking work and involved the total co-operation of the elected Indian church officials. Although the people of Anaham, and in due course other Chilcotin bands, showed interest in Christianity and responded well to Father

Thomas and the implementation of the Durieu System, they were far from being regarded as Catholic Indians. Under the Durieu System not even baptism, which required a year's probation, was regarded as proof of conversion. As is evident by a letter to Father LeJacq, Bishop Durieu recognized the possibility of Indian self-interest motivating the desire for baptism:

> To a missionary who finds this work of continually watching and destroying too crude and humiliating, experience teaches that without it the result is pagans whitewashed by baptism, continuing to live as they lived of old, cloaking their evil lives under the mantle of religious hypocrisy! It is a truism that the Indian quickly brings his religion in accord with actions that flatter his self-interest and passion . . . the Indians, although baptized, saying their prayers, and even confessing, very often retain within their hearts pagan ideas and maxims which will often be the norm of their daily actions.[8]

In a second letter to Father LeJacq, Durieu went on at length and in great detail to explain the methods by which the missionary, after instilling in the Indians fear of God and of disobeying the Commandments, could "fire the Indians' hearts" with a fervent desire to receive the sacrament of Holy Communion. Indians wishing to receive this sacrament had to ask the missionary formally. They then underwent a year or more of probation during which time they were watched over, instructed, tested, and reprimanded by an Indian watchman especially chosen for this work. He was known as "the watchman of Jesus Christ." During the years of preparation — the actual time period was decided by the zeal of the candidate — the Indians had to show their respect and love for Jesus by frequent visits to the church, by constant assistance at all the religious exercises, catechism sessions, and prayer meetings, both during and outside of regular priest-attended missions, by guarding themselves against temptation to sin through devotion to Durieu's rules, and by putting their trust in their appointed watchman, "seeking him out and lovingly practising his recommendations."[9]

These are just a selection of the measures that Bishop Durieu insisted upon before the Indians could receive communion and among the Chilcotins, as with all the Cariboo's Indians, Father Thomas followed Durieu's instructions to the letter. Like his mentor, François Thomas was well aware that the Indians, while claiming to believe in the Church's teaching, still participated in "pagan feasts" and, in later years, drinking parties. Each mission, which came to be known as "priest time," was also the occasion for horse races, an attraction said to have been "permitted" by Paul Durieu, but which could have been the major drawing card for some Indians. Consequently, thirteen years passed from the time that the Chilcotins of Anaham organized until Father Thomas gave Communion to the first Indians of this band — three adults and four children. From that time on however the numbers increased yearly and other Chilcotin villages began to present themselves as candidates for the sacrament. As proof of the increase, the Report of the Vicariate for 1898 and 1918, recorded that the number of Communions distributed by Father Thomas rose from 600 per annum in 1898 to 4,000 yearly in 1918. According to Father Thomas this was the "Golden Age" at Anaham and other Chilcotin reserves.

Another measure of Indian commitment to their new religion can be seen in their attitude towards church-building. Father Thomas was determined to keep alive the enthusiasm generated by the blessing of the Sugar Cane church. By 1897, the original log chapels in Indian villages had become rather dilapidated. Several new churches were needed, particularly among the Chilcotin and the Carriers. But it was among the Shuswap at Canoe Creek that Father Thomas began his campaign to build not just a replacement log church but a church built on the European model. He also changed the pattern of a missionary sleeping in the chief's house by "insisting" that a cabin be built for the priest alongside the church. "I had no personal objection to sleeping in an Indian cabin or under a tree" explained Father Thomas, "but I felt that, as many came to the Priest with their problems, it would be better for all concerned if the Priest had a little log cabin of his own." The Indians acquiesced. The church at Canoe Creek was in such a state that snow and wind blew in between the logs. $2500 was needed to raise a church and a cabin. Before calling a general meeting of the whole village to discuss the issue, the missionary spoke confidentially to those he considered "the more sensible" Indians, going over with them the pros and cons of the undertaking. He also visited an Indian "who had great influence and was fairly well off" but opposed to spending time and money on a new church, in order to gain his support. At the ensuing general meeting, all the men promised to donate twenty-five dollars each towards the church and the women promised five dollars each. Some offered animals and farm products, and Annette, the Chief's wife, promised to give every calf born of her cow until the church was paid for. Tougan, an eighty-five year old man, donated his only horse, saying, "if I help build a house for God here at Canoe Creek, the good God will give me His own house in Heaven." William Waspuilor, who was elected manager of the undertaking, cleared a field, seeded and cultivated it, and donated the crop to the building fund. Jimmy Brown, a Métis carpenter who had been educated by the Oblates at New Westminster, was given the contract. After these preliminaries were completed, the Canoe Creek Indians sent a delegation to their friends at Canim Lake to ask permission to trap for two months on their hunting ground. Not only was permission granted but a number of Canim Lake Indians helped in the trapping. The Indians decided that all the animals which they had trapped, except those caught in the last two weeks, would be sold for the benefit of the new church. They repeated this procedure the following year and succeeded in raising enough money for both buildings. The Propagation of the Faith and the Oblate Community provided money to build pews "not unworthy of a parish church in France."

In 1902, Bishop Augustine Dontenwill, who succeeded to the Vicariate on the death of Paul Durieu in 1899, and Fathers LeJeune and Chirouse Jr. all officiated at the blessing of the new church which had all the pomp and pageantry of previous events. The Indians constructed a meeting house made of trees and branches large enough to accommodate the local Indians and their numerous guests. A huge cross carried by eight Indians was erected, there was a torchlight procession of the Blessed Sacrament, and processions in honour of the Blessed Virgin and St. Joseph. During the ceremonies, the Bishop confirmed fifty Indians, a figure that was indicative of the religious progress among the Indians of St. Joseph's Mission district. The mission closed with a general communion, then "everyone shook hands with everybody else and, full of happiness and legitimate pride at the success of the religious gathering, the eight hundred returned home." It is interesting to note that, in 1884, the local Indian Agent had considered the Canoe Creek band "the least promising tribe" in his agency.

The new churches built on other reservations were financed, erected, and blessed in the same way — "except for the fact that, as time went on, the ceremonies and religious celebrations may have been a little more elaborate." In 1901, Bishop Dontenwill blessed St. Paul's Church at Quesnel, confirming both Quesnel and Kluskuz Lake Indians. The Bishop arrived on a large barge decorated with boughs and flowers and filled with Indians singing hymns composed in the Carrier language. A new church at Alexandria was built by Indian money earned through trapping or working for white men. The Alexandria chief, Chief Sam, exhorted his people to donate generously: "I know that I must have spent $1,000 on whiskey. Many of you have done the same. Let us now give money to build a church and let us do so generously." In 1904 the local Indians of Quesnel moved to a new reservation which they called Egypt. There a temporary log church was erected. Six years later a new church was built from the sale of furs and by collecting fifty cents from each of the numerous visitors who attended the blessing of the church. The enthusiasm for church building was not limited to the Shuswap and Carrier. Having committed themselves to Christianity the Chilcotin also engaged in church building but, as the missionaries had come to expect, they were built in "Chilcotin time." By 1923, the Indians had financed a new church at Anaham, but they had first planned the project in 1908. They had placed Captain Bobby, an Indian catechist, in charge of fund raising. Initially they erected a cabin for the missionary at a cost of $200 and Tommy Lemdrum who had been commissioned to build the church, lived in the cabin during construction. The church was expected to cost over a thousand dollars and, as cash was in short supply, each family donated a horse towards expenses. In 1921, "a good number of Anaham people," leading sixty horses, met Father Thomas at Nazko and the group set out for Kluskuz Lake and Elgatcho, some 175 miles distant. By selling these horses to their fur-trapping neighbours the Elgatcho, whose horses had been killed by a severe winter and lack of hay, the church was furnished with "a beautiful confessional" which was sent from Vancouver at a cost of $120, an elaborate altar railing, statues of Mary and St. Joseph, a sanctuary lamp and a holy water font. In a spirit of co-operation, a new altar was built by two Shuswap Indians from Alkali Lake. The blessing ceremonies, presided over by Bishop Bunoz, was an imitation of Bishop Durieu's ceremonies at the blessing of Sugar Cane church in 1895. Nine hundred people, Chilcotin, Shuswap, and local whites attended the ceremonies, and "as a sign of the friendship now existing between the two former enemies," 185 Chilcotin and 40 Shuswap were confirmed together. The revival spirit was being maintained.

Like his predecessors, Father Thomas was involved in the material as well as spiritual well-being of Cariboo's Indians. In his *Memoirs*, the missionary makes several references to his involvement in obtaining reserve land. One reference is not very explicit: "Taking Father LeJacq's advice, I had obtained 2,000 acres of good land for the Kluskuz Indians and they built a nice little church (St. John's) there." No further details are given. The missionary is more specific about his aid to the Alexis Creek Indians. These people were living in the woods because a white man had pre-empted their land. In the spring of 1902, Chief Sam of Alexis Creek, who had been baptized by Father LeJacq, sent for Father Thomas to visit a sick Indian. The missionary invited the people to Anaham where at the end of June a large gathering of Indians would participate in a mission. At that time, Father Thomas advised the Alexis Indians to choose a site for a reserve, promising to persuade the government to give them their chosen area.

The Indians chose Redstone and the missionary then advised them to build there some cabins for themselves and a larger one to serve as a chapel, meeting room, and living quarters for the missionaries. By the winter, five cabins had been erected but, according to Father Thomas, there had been no time to fill the gaps between the logs, and as the chapel had no stove the first religious service "wasn't very amusing." Over the years, the population at Redstone grew considerably. Adding his petition to that of the local Indian Agent H. E. Taylor, and government surveyor D. J. Mackay, the missionary helped to persuade the government to give Redstone Plateau to the Indians. As the Plateau had no water for irrigation, the missionary wrote another petition requesting good hay meadows for every family and the government complied. Inadequate water supplies was a grave problem for many Indian bands. More often than not, land with water or easy access to water had been preempted by whites and, as Father McGuckin had noted years earlier, it would take a great deal of money to provide the Indians with adequate irrigation systems. The village of Anaham had a water supply nearby but according to Father Thomas it was "bad water." Consequently the Indians had to travel a considerable distance to get usable drinking water. The missionary spoke to Dr. Wright, the Minister of Health, who promised to obtain the pipes and pumps necessary to bring the clean water to the village. The government granted $200 for the project and, in 1927, the Indians began to dig out the necessary six-foot ditch; a year later the system was functioning well.

By virtue of his sixty years' work at the Mission and his unceasing journeys throughout the Cariboo, Father Thomas became a well-known and well-liked missionary among the area's white population, many of whom are willing to bear testimony to his total dedication to his work. In the history of the Mission, he represented a return to the early days of total dedication to the Indians' spiritual welfare; he was Bishop Durieu's last, and possibly most dedicated, disciple.

NOTES TO CHAPTER VII

[1] Fisher, *Contact and Conflict*, p. 127.

[2] Besson, *Un Missionaire d'Autrefois*, p. 174.

[3] All the information regarding this and the preceding event is to be found in Father LeJacq to Superior General, October 21, 1895, Manuscript, O.A.

[4] Information quoted throughout this chapter regarding the life and work of Father Thomas is taken from "Memoirs."

[5] Letter of Father George Forbes, March 30, 1957, to unknown subject. Uncatalogued Documents, St. Joseph's Mission, Williams Lake.

[6] Fisher, *Contact and Conflict*, p. 199.

[7] *Missions de la Congregation des Missionaires Oblate de Marie Immaculee, 1883*, Paris, 1862-1900, p. 356 — referred to hereafter as *Missions*.

[8] Bishop Paul Durieu to Father LeJacq, November 27, 1883, File No. HE 1791, D96C, A.D.

[9] Durieu to Father LeJacq, February 25, 1884, File No. HE 1791, D96C, A.D.

The arrival of the Sisters of the Child Jesus.

Chapter VIII

"THE MISSION"

To several generations of the Cariboo's Indians, the Mission had meant simply the Mission school. Since the opening of St. Joseph's, the Indians had been promised education for their children and Paul Durieu, who had always seen the necessity for Indian schools at the Mission, intended to make good that promise. In the spring of 1890, Bishop Durieu wrote to Francis James Barnard, M.P. for Yale-Cariboo district, on the desirability of an Indian industrial boarding school at Williams Lake. As hunters, fishermen and stock-raisers, the Indians of the Cariboo had always lived off the land, but Bishop Durieu was convinced that they needed training in European agricultural pursuits:

> ... being untrained they are unable to derive a real advantage from the cultivation of their land and the rearing of cattle. Whence it happens that every year we find so many destitute amongst them, how great a boon an Industrial and Boarding school would be both to the young Indians and their parents who would benefit by the knowledge acquired by their children after their return to the Reserve.

The Bishop suggested that the best place for such an establishment in the Cariboo region was St. Joseph's Mission, as the Mission site was in fact selected "so as to be fitted for an Industrial School for Indians."[1]

In recommending that education, particularly education combined with agricultural training, would help the Indians to adjust to their more restricted living situation, Paul Durieu was reiterating a point of view that had been held in North America as early as 1743. In that year an American missionary, the Reverend John Sergeant, had suggested that Indian educational institutions should divide the Indians' time between study and manual work. A farm attached to each school would provide the opportunity for farm work and also "sustain the scholars." In 1803, the American Presbyterian General Assembly supported a school among the Cherokees where Indian children were to become "beacons by which the parents might gradually be conducted into the same field of improvement."[2] In 1819, the American Secretary of War, John C. Calhoun, established a fund for Indian education but it was to support only those undertakings which stressed "agriculture and mechanical arts" for Indian boys and "spinning, weaving, and sewing for girls."[3]

In Canada the theory that the Indians would benefit by education and agricultural knowledge was followed with equal determination. As early as 1676, on the site of present-day Montreal, the Sulphician Order established an Industrial school for the Indians. In southern Ontario, Methodist missionaries in the 1820's and 1830's demonstrated the arts of cultivation to the Indians; manual labour schools at Alderville and Muncey had model farm equipped to teach Indian children how to farm.[4] In 1847, G. Vardon, then Assistant Superintendent General of Indian Affairs, asked Methodist leader Dr. Egerton Ryerson for his suggestions on the best method of establishing and conducting industrial schools for the benefit of the Indians. Ryerson replied:

> ... in respect to intellectual training give a plain English education adapted to the working farmer and mechanic... but in addition to this, pupils of the industrial schools are to be taught agriculture, kitchen gardening, and mechanics, so far as mechanics is connected with making and repairing the most useful agricultural implements.

In the same vein Paul Durieu wrote to Barnard that the Indian girls attending the Mission would be instructed "in the management of a dairy as well as in every other branch of housekeeping," while the Indian boys would be taught "everything pertaining to the business of the farm, so as to fit them for management of their own farms."

To Indian policymakers the idea of residential industrial schools was eminently practical and, of course, economical, as one establishment could take in students from a large geographical area; but to the Churches there were other important considerations. Until as late as the 1950's, Indian residential schools were regarded as "the ideal set-up" for retaining and strengthening the Catholic faith, and this was the Oblates' primary concern.[5] Ideally a day school on each reserve would have provided the necessary formal education, with agricultural training being given on the Indians' own land. But even if the Churches — that is all Churches involved in Indian education — had had the finances necessary to build and staff the many schools needed, they would still have preferred the boarding school situation. Like other denominations, the Oblates deemed it necessary to separate the children from their home environment so that they could be trained as good Christian young people, on the European model. At St. Joseph's, Father Thomas, and later on his assistants, would continue travelling the Cariboo providing the Indians with the opportunity for religious services and instruction; but the Mission school established by Bishop Durieu would provide Indian children with a totally religious environment and, somewhat ironically, a totally different approach to religious instruction. The children were to be treated as Catholic European children and learn to accept their religion as a way of life.

As a member of the staff, Bishop Durieu had observed the success of the Indian residential industrial schools which the Oblates had opened for boys and girls at St. Mary's Mission in 1867 and 1870 respectively. Confident that the concept of the residential school ensured a sound Catholic and "civilizing" education for Indian children, the Oblates, under Durieu's direction, opened a government-supported Indian residential school at Cranbrook in 1889, and a second at Kamloops in 1890. In response to Bishop Durieu's suggestion of another establishment at the Mission, A. G. Vowell, Federal Indian Superintendent in Victoria, asked local Indian Agent William L. Meason to examine the property. In his initial report, Meason stated that the location of the Mission site was suitable for a school as it was "sufficiently isolated" from the nearest settlement and wagon road. In a further more detailed report the following April, Meason wrote that the Mission land was "of good quality" but that it might be necessary to construct another building as the present ones were not large enough to accommodate many students. However he again stressed the suitability of the locale in terms of its isolation which suggests that the Department of Indian Affairs subscribed to the notion that segregation from populated areas was highly desirable. In the previous February, Meason had inquired under what terms Bishop Durieu would sell the two Mission school buildings to the department. This time however the Bishop was not prepared to sell Oblate property to the government. He submitted a proposition whereby the Church would operate the proposed schools:

I propose to use all the buildings of St. Joseph's for the Industrial School, and undertake to manage and run it with the Rev. Fathers and the Sisters of Charity [the Sisters of St. Ann] for the capitation grant of $130 per annum for each Indian pupil if allowance is made the first year for fifty children. We will give them board, clothing, care, education and training in two or three trades, the Government being at no further expense than the capitation grant.

As the future was to reveal, this contract was to prove detrimental to the Mission.

Paul Durieu was not always a good businessman. Taking the advice of Father Emmelen (who later left the Oblates to become a secular priest), Bishop Durieu exchanged the extremely valuable Oblate property in the Okanagan for shares in what turned out to be a worthless gold-mine in California. Now he offered the government a contract which left many financial responsibilities in the hands of the Oblates. The contract initially appeared to be equally favourable to both parties. It called for a nine-part agreement, the government to provide a per capita grant, to arrange the curriculum (half a day's instruction in academic subjects and the remainder of the day given to trade training), to select the trades to be taught, to decide which children would attend, to inspect the schools, and to exercise authority to fire unsatisfactory teachers. The Bishop was to hire the staff "including a carpenter and blacksmith," and provide religious education for the children. Desiring to retain ownership of the land and buildings and, perhaps through this, minimize government control, Bishop Durieu left the responsibility of maintaining the buildings and property in the hands of the Oblates. The Department of Indian Affairs quickly accepted this generous offer and, on May 11, 1891, the Department's Chief Clerk requested the government to insert in the supplementary estimates for 1891-1892, a capitation grant of $130 for fifty Indian children for the new industrial school to be opened at the Mission.

Bishop Durieu's first task was to find teachers for the new schools. The Bishop fully expected the Sisters of St. Ann to return to the Mission. When forced to close down their girls' school, the Sisters had indicated that they would return if conditions changed: "it is not without regret that we have finally come to the decision of withdrawing our Sisters from this mission and waiting for better days. We shall be happy to return to this field of labour. As soon as the number of children increases, we will find work there."[6] With this letter to Bishop D'herbomez before him, Paul Durieu had little doubt that he could count on the Sisters. In April 1890, they had willingly accepted his offer to run the Kamloops Indian Residential School which had opened under the temporary direction of Catholic lay personnel. Writing to express his happiness at their decision, he took the opportunity to inform the Sisters that the federal government had "made it almost certain" that St. Joseph's would be chosen for an industrial school and asked about their plans to return there.[7]

The Sisters of St. Ann however were "very hard pressed to answer the needs of existing work" and, to the Bishop's dismay their General Council stated categorically, "we have refused, we refuse, and we shall refuse, for some time, all requests for foundations." Sister Mary Providence in Victoria added that perhaps the delay was not really an inconvenience as the school buildings were far from being ready. As Bishop Durieu was not prepared to wait, he began proceedings to buy back the Sister's property at St. Joseph's for the sum of $1250, and opened negotiations with the Sisters of Providence in Oregon. After agreeing to take up the new work, providing they could have the $130 per pupil given by the government, the Sisters of Providence once again changed their mind and decided they could not take on the responsibility of an Indian school for girls at the Mission.[8] The religious orders were apparently having difficulty keeping up with the demand for their services in the expanding communities of the West. Determined to open the girls' school without delay, Bishop Durieu decided to hire lay people until he could find an order of nuns for the work. Meanwhile he appointed Father LeJacq principal of the boys' school and began efforts to find lay teachers for both academic subjects and the trades. On July 14, 1891, the Bishop wrote to Vowell: "We are ready to open the Industrial School at Williams Lake. We will receive this month as many boys as we may find willing to come in at this season of the year." The Indians finally had their school, but they responded reluctantly.

The Chiefs of the Cariboo, who in earlier days had sought out new educational opportunities for their children, had certainly not visualized handing the young Indians over to the complete care of the Church. While the Chiefs realized that outsiders would necessarily be involved in teaching their children "the new mysteries," they intended the new learning to be a supplement to, not a replacement for, traditional education. By the time the Mission was willing to receive Indian children many years had passed in which, with the possible exception of some remote groups, the Cariboo's people had had to come to terms with the permanent presence of the whites. The land was no longer theirs. They returned to familiar summer camps to find fencing enclosing their land. While some compassionate men, including some of their missionaries, tried to help them fight a self-serving white government, the Indians struggled to come to grips with the new reality. Some made the adjustment, many did not. Now, after suffering a loss of land, loss of traditional tribal government, loss of social patterns, and the loss of a lifestyle dependent only on nature, the Indians were asked to give up their children.

Initially they had a choice as it was not until 1895 that education became compulsory for Indian children between the age of seven and sixteen. They could keep their children close to ensure continuity with the past or they could send them away to gain new knowledge which might help both children and parents to understand and survive the new order. There was another consideration. The children, particularly the boys, were often vital to the family economy. Bishop Durieu had good reason to expect a low attendance when the school opened in mid-summer in direct competition with fishing, hunting, farming, and stock raising activities. He was confident however that the choice of St. Joseph's as a school would meet with Indian approval; "the Indians, who are all Catholics, would hail with delight the selection of the Mission as the site of the Schools as they are accustomed to assemble from time to time around their missionaries." Whether it was simply the wrong time of the year, as Durieu suspected, or a reluctance on the part of the Indians to make the commitment, the Mission School opened with only twelve pupils — a far cry from the hundreds that Father McGuckin had anticipated. But, as Superintendent Vowell pointed out, this was advantageous as the school had the opportunity to "thoroughly attend to and particularly instruct them as to a knowledge of the English language and discipline"; this first group could then instruct later ones "in English, rules, and regulations."

Initially all went smoothly. The school received adequate quarterly cheques from Ottawa and the numbers of children quickly increased. The Bishop, after attending a General Chapter of the Congregation in France, went to his home in Le Puy where he visited the Mother House of the Sisters of the Child Jesus. There he began negotiations with Reverend Mother Alphonsine to establish a congregation in British Columbia. Meanwhile, a capable Catholic woman, who had taught at Kamloops before the Sisters of St. Ann took over, managed the girls' school. The first problem encountered involved the staffing of the boys' school.

Paul Durieu did not want a repetition of past years when so many Oblates at the Mission had lived as school teachers. He wanted an Oblate principal but he preferred to use lay people as teachers and disciplinarians. The problem was getting reliable Catholic male teachers to come to the wilderness area of the Cariboo. As Bishop Dontenwill wrote to Superintendent Vowell:

> We have to labour under heavy odds in a district which is hard and expensive to reach and in which a man accustomed to the social conditions elsewhere finds it still harder to live. Hence when a young man has realize[d] a little money, he returns to civilization.

The temptation to drink was often irresistable in isolated areas, and frontier schools throughout North America attracted men of uncertain character. The Mission School was no exception. Finding men of good character willing to work with the Indian children at the Mission was an impossible task.

The school was open for a year before the Bishop found either a suitable blacksmith or carpenter to teach industrial skills. In September 1892 the Oblates engaged Patrick MacCarrill, a blacksmith who could "turn his hand to anything" including farming and carpenter work. He became the school's "Master of Trades." The man seemed promising but would only sign a one-year contract and the following year he demanded an increase which the Mission could not afford. His place was taken by a Mr. Horan who, although a satisfactory employee in many respects, "would not abandon his pretensions to do as he pleased." However, he worked at the school for three years before Father LeJacq dismissed him for ignoring the Principal's advice and taking "too active a part in electioneering." As a replacement could not be found, Horan was re-hired but his second term was marked by a series of offences against the school. He took three months leave of absence in 1901, leading the Principal to believe he had the permission of the Indian Agent when he had not; the following year he was "drunk and disorderly" at 150 Mile House, an action which threatened the school's reputation, and he got into debt, which was considered "discreditable to an employee of the School which paid him a good salary."

In addition to the disquieting behaviour of staff, another more serious problem began to plague the school. The much-needed government cheques began to arrive late. "It will be impossible for me to run the machine" protested the irate Superior "if the government is delaying so long to send in the cheque." Then, in 1893, Superintendent Vowell advised an astonished Father LeJacq that the per capita grant would be given for twenty-five students rather than fifty. Vowell explained that although the Indian department had recommended payment for fifty pupils, that number was reduced to twenty-five in Cabinet. Angered by the department's stance, Father LeJacq suggested to the Council of the Vicariate that the Oblates should "put the government on the spot" by threatening to close the school until the allocation for fifty children was re-established. Aware that the government could call upon another denomination to take over if the Oblates should refuse to operate the school, the Council decided to be prudent. While regretting the situation, the Council advised Father LeJacq that it would be "very difficult to force the government to re-establish the allocation considering that the whole business had been proposed and promised by the agent of the government and never voted by the Chambers." The Oblates apparently felt that in making an agreement with them, Superintendent Vowell may have overstepped his authority.[9] The Council agreed to arrive at a solution by negotiation and, as a temporary measure, to cut expenses by closing the girls' department.

Already expenses were becoming a major problem. The girls' school building was in poor condition. The Sisters of St. Ann had never had sufficient cash to keep up with repairs and it had stood empty and totally neglected for three years. The Oblates estimated that it stood in need of several thousand dollars worth of repairs and renovations. The boys' building, which contained the Mission living quarters, was in better condition but it was considered too old and too small for efficient management. In addition to running repairs, the Oblates had had to provide cash for beds and bedding, and necessary workshops and tools for vocational training in blacksmithing, carpentry, and shoe and harness making. The Bishop protested to the Indian Department that he was obliged to keep two separate school staffs, maintain both buildings and pay two cooks. Eventually a compromise was reached. The government agreed to pay for thirty-five pupils and granted $2,000 towards the construction of a new boys' school. When, in the spring of 1894, the government sent a quarterly cheque for only $756, Bishop Durieu threatened to close the girls' school permanently unless the government kept to its agreement.[10]

Although financially the future of the girls' department looked uncertain, Paul Durieu continued negotiations with the Sisters of the Child Jesus, and in the spring of 1896 Sister Aimée de Maria, who was made Superior, and Sisters Euphrasia, Saint-Fabian and Félician, all of whom "had begged to come to the West of Canada,"[11] were appointed to British Columbia. The Sisters left Le Puy on April 28, 1896. They sailed to New York, then left by train for British Columbia via Montreal. They were met at Ashcroft on May 17th by Bishop Durieu who had come to escort them to the Mission.[12] Sister Félician kept a diary of their journey and her words indicate that the journey to the Mission had not improved much since the Sisters of St. Ann travelled the road twenty years earlier.

> We stepped into the stagecoach, a heavy vehicle in which His Excellency seated himself after having helped four little missionaries embarrassed at finding themselves the object of so much solicitude. At first we had laughed at the repeated jolts on the road which reminded us of Lafontaine's expression about roads as uneven as washboards. But this was more like a trail packed down by the passage of all manner of vehicles rigged up to serve as stagecoaches. I had at first greeted these jolts with peals of laughter, but there is a limit to everything. And this wagon equipped with benches bounced on from bump to bump, sinking its wheels into deep ruts, unable to go any faster in spite of the fierce will of the ten horses which pulled us at a dizzy speed through poplar woods and over rough trails.

The missionaries and the Indians accorded the French nuns a warm and ceremonious welcome but Sister Felician almost ruined the solemnity of the occasion. She was inclined to laugh uncontrollably at the most inappropriate times and, in spite of a request by the Bishop that she "put on a grave exterior," Sister Félician struggled throughout the proceedings fighting "a wild desire to laugh." After shaking hands with the adults, the Sisters made themselves known to the thirty little Indian girls who would share their rather delapidated convent-schoolhouse. If the solemn-faced Indian children appeared strange to the French nuns, the oddly clothed Sisters appeared totally alien to the Indian children. Communication was out of the question. The Shuswap, Carrier, and Chilcotin children all spoke different languages. The Sisters spoke only French. As lessons had to be given in English, both teachers and pupils had to learn a new language. The efforts of her fellow companions to master English often caused Sister Félician's "merciless urge to laugh" to overpower her.

It was vital to have a good sense of humour in those early days as conditions were still primitive. Sister Félician commented on the great discomfort the nuns experienced when winter set in:

> In vain did we run around to keep warm; we shivered and our teeth chattered uncontrollably. The refectory was the coldest. The stove roared until we thought the chimney was on fire, yet the room remained icy. The meat, milk, coffee, everything was frozen, and Sister Saint-Fabian had to summon all her strength to cut the beef steak which was like rock. In cooling, the dishes stuck to the table. The nights were frigid.

The older boys and girls and the Oblate Brothers spent time every day cutting and stacking sufficient wood to keep both buildings heated. In spite of these difficult conditions, two years passed before the Indian Department could be persuaded to donate the $2,000 necessary for improvements to the girls' school. The boys fared better as, in 1896, the government gave the promised $2,000 towards a new boys' building.

Initially the Sisters taught only the girls but, within a year, they had a new role when Bishop Durieu further strengthened the role of St. Joseph's as an Indian mission by establishing there the first Indian novitiate. A novitiate, a place where under the direction of religious personnel, young girls (or young men) spent a probationary period preparing for admittance into a religious order, had long been Paul Durieu's dream. In May 1897, after travelling from New Westminster with Father Thomas, four Indian girls from the Stalo tribe of the lower Fraser Valley arrived at St. Joseph's. They had been educated at St. Mary's Mission by the Sisters of St. Ann and desired to become teaching nuns. The Bishop arranged with the Sisters of the Child Jesus to accept the girls for their six-month probationary period. During that time one of the Sisters, who was appointed their novice mistress, studied the sincerity of the girls' interest in religious life and their physical, mental, and spiritual fitness.

"They were good girls," wrote Father Thomas to a fellow Oblate, "but I suppose that they were lonesome and they persevered only five or six months and then went home to their reserves."[13] No local girls attended the novitiate during its brief lifespan although, when the Sisters of the Child Jesus opened a novitiate for white girls at Sechelt in 1911, a Shuswap girl completed her novitiate there. She was then sent to a convent in North Battleford, Saskatchewan. She died in St. Albert in 1918 during the influenza epidemic. Although she "persevered," Father Thomas concluded that Sister Henrietta "was perhaps not as happy in religious life as a white girl might have been." Despite its failure, the novitiate at St. Joseph's was a mark of Paul Durieu's confidence in the spiritual progress of the Indians.

For several years the Sisters continued to teach only the girls, but this had to change. The Oblates were still unable to obtain quality staff for the boys' department, although every attempt was made to pick men who were suitable. Mr. Bridges, hired as an academic teacher in September 1900, resigned his position the following June "giving for reasons that he could better his position." In spite of this, two years later in 1902, he wrote letters to Father Boening (who became principal when cancer hospitalized Father LeJacq in 1898), "couched in the most friendly language" and begged to be taken back as a teacher or "in any capacity." As, soon after his departure, he had "commenced to make serious charges" against the management of the school, his overtures were rejected. In the hopes of reversing the situation Bishop Durieu turned to the East and "purposely" hired two men from Ottawa, Mr. Brophy and Mr. Fahy. Mr. Brophy "did very well" until Christmas when "he disgraced himself twice" by going to the 150 Mile House, the second time without permission, "and there gambled and intoxicated himself." Because of the scandal, particularly because of the bad example to the Indians, Brophy was dismissed. The use of lay people was clearly not working and in 1902, under the direction of Bishop Dontenwill, the Oblates recognized their dependency on religious staff and replaced most of the laymen. Oblate Brothers took over the roles of carpenter-instructor and disciplinarian, and two Sisters of the Child Jesus were employed to teach academic subjects to the boys. Mr. Fahy was retained as agricultural instructor.

Although the staff situation was now resolved, other problems persisted. From the day it opened its doors, the Mission School came under attack. Mr. Barnard, M.P., who had been instrumental in bringing Bishop Durieu's idea for an Indian residential school in the Cariboo to the attention of the federal government, expressed his concern that "contrary to protestations made by him at various times" the school was placed completely under the control of the Catholic Church. Federal Superintendent General Vankoughnet explained that as the federal government's official returns showed all the Indians at Williams Lake to be Catholic, "no question ever arose" of putting the school under other than Catholic Church control. While the reasons for Barnard's protest remain unknown — although he could have been protesting on behalf of constituents — the reason for the hostility towards the new establishment of some of the local settlers is quite clear. They saw the school as a threat to their livelihood.

The first complaint arose in 1894, by which time the school was fairly well established. Local businessman R. V. Davison complained to Barnard (who in turn complained to Ottawa) that the school manufactured goods "at penitentiary prices," providing unfair competition for local businessmen and undermining his harness business. Father LeJacq denied that the school wanted "to run opposition to anybody" but it needed an outlet for the articles manufactured by the Indian boys in their industrial classes. M. Scott, Deputy Indian Superintendent in Ottawa, agreed that this was a reasonable and a common practice and that because of insufficient government funding such schools had to sell the products of the trades taught "to provide sufficient revenue." Although an investigation revealed that Davison's complaints were "without foundation," the accusations continued and became more virulent.

One list of complaints in 1899 led the Superintendent of Indian Affairs to direct Vowell and local Indian Agent Bell to inspect the Mission School and make full independent reports of the situation they found. The two inspectors visited the school "without having notified the School authorities of their intention to inspect it." In separate reports, they exonerated the school of all charges. Contrary to the charge that the Oblates took in white children and "half-breeds," the men found none at the school. White children did in fact attend the school, which was the only one in the district, but they were day students only, riding to the Mission each morning and returning home in the evening. The Oblates had been accused of teaching only one trade but were, in reality, teaching harness-making (which explains Mr. Davison's chagrin), farming, milking, dairying and gardening. Someone accused the school of keeping the children "dirty and not properly clothed" but both inspectors reported the children and staff to be clean and well fed. To the surprise of both men, the Indian children could answer questions "more readily" than many white children in the common schools they had visited. The government officials also concluded that although the harness shop was "carried on a paying basis," the cuts in prices did not interfere with other local products. After the inspection, Vowell called on the Bishop and suggested he hire a man to teach carpentry; Durieu assured him "that what the Department most desired would be attended."

These reports did nothing to assuage the unpopularity of the school. Whether through an aversion to the Indians or to the religious order, many local residents who opposed the institution continued their complaints and even claimed that the coming of the Indian Agent or of Vowell was known to the staff beforehand. In July 1900, E. A. Carew-Gibson of 150 Mile House complained to Vowell that the school had established a large warehouse and blacksmith shop. In addition, Carew-Gibson charged the Mission with running a harness shop and butcher shop, and with using their religion "to secure cheap labour and other assistance." Apparently to the annoyance of local business establishments, entrepreneurism was still flourishing at the Mission. Another investigation was made and the charges were declared unfounded. "Carew-Gibson" declared an Ottawa official, "must have been misled by the representations of highly-prejudiced parties."

Because of further complaints received in Ottawa — one from Mr. Bridges, the former teacher at the Mission — about ill-fed and ill-treated Indian children, the department telegraphed Vowell on April 12, 1902, to make a full inquiry into the school's management. To insure that the Mission was unaware of his intention to visit, Vowell remained at 150 Mile House until after 5 p.m. on the evening of April 24, and then drove quietly to the school "so as to arrive in time to find the children at their evening meal." Vowell found the food to be "good and wholesome" although, since it was Lent, "they had no meat." After speaking privately with the children and visiting Alkali Lake reserve to question parents, Vowell concluded that the children were well cared for, but that the use of corporal punishment as a form of discipline needed to be modified.

In reporting his findings to Ottawa, Vowell again raised the issue of local hostility. After describing how the school planned to resume instruction of older boys "in practical gardening," the Superintendent explained that the program had been discontinued the previous year principally because the boys were too small for agricultural work; however, there was a secondary factor. Local settlers and storekeepers had complained that the Mission was using the children as cheap labour. Vowell commented that this was an "erroneous impression" because the marginal work done by the older pupils "could not reasonably be considered as a factor in the economic working of the Mission land." The Superintendent concluded that his inspection had let the Oblates understand "that their actions in the conduct of the School were under close observation"; it had also given confidence to both the children and the Indian parents that the department was looking after the children's interests.

Everyone claimed to have the children's interests at heart. Both the Church and government representatives were convinced that the program of education at the Mission would benefit the Indians. The priests, brothers, nuns, and Indian agents knew only one form of education: a tightly controlled, frequently harsh, educational regime imported from Europe. Schools operated under strict controls. School staff expected order, instant obedience, total attentiveness, and disciplined behaviour. If a child failed to act according to the expected norm, or exhibited behavioural problems, the answer was punishment. This system of education, applied in all schools, public, private, and parochial, had the support of parents who themselves had experienced the same. This European system was applied at the Mission without any consideration being given to cultural clash. An Indian child was simply a child.

It was never considered necessary to alter the system to accommodate children whose personality traits included concentrating on and enjoying the present and, although under advice from elders, exercising personal freedom of choice.[14] The Indian child, who had never been confined for long periods of time, who had been educated in the closeness of the extended family group, and who had seldom, if ever, been physically punished for his misdeeds, was expected to accommodate himself to his new environment. Just as Indian parents were unlikely to understand Father LeJacq's commonly held belief that fear was the beginning of wisdom, Indian children were unlikely to understand that even the most patient or sympathetic teacher saw value in the use of corporal punishment. Nor would the Indians have thought too highly of local Indian Agent Daunt's view that "the lower you go in the human strata the more delicate the susceptibility apparently becomes, and what would not appear out of the way to a Duke's son in the way of discipline would entail great hardship and outrage upon that of the working man or an Indian."

The reaction of the Mission schoolchildren to a totally alien environment was as varied as the personalities of the children themselves. Among the children, as among children everywhere, there was the bold and the timid, the adventuresome and the fearful, the curious and the uninterested, the pliable and the stubborn. Some like David and Celestine Johnson of Alkali Lake, who went to the Mission in 1906 and 1905 respectively, "didn't mind" going to school but they had no idea what that entailed.[15] Celestine could not understand why her parents left her. Like most of their contemporaries, neither David nor Celestine spoke or understood English. They did not even know what "yes" was! Celestine, who was too small to begin regular lessons, remembers spending her first months helping the cook. Some Indian children were anxious to go to school. Amelia Dick had to persuade the aunt who raised her to let her go; "I told them to put me in," she recalls, "as I was a nuisance around here." David Belleau "hated" the school and "couldn't count" the number of times he ran away.

Running away was the most common and most consistent way in which the children of the Cariboo expressed their dissatisfaction with the Mission School. Even for adventurous children, there was a limit to the novelty value of a school uniform (with Sunday shoes that pinched), a daily routine controlled by bells, and hours spent in classrooms learning the basics of reading and writing. They could not understand why the boys went into one building and the girls into another. Some visiting between brothers and sisters was allowed, particularly when parents visited the Mission, and the "Indian parlour" was the scene of many tearful reunions and partings. Sometimes the Indians would camp near the school and children visited parents during recreation time. But in school, the only time the boys and girls were together was in chapel where they occupied opposite sides of the building. This challenged the resourcefulness of the boys, some of whom resorted to the use of small hand mirrors to achieve a forbidden look at the opposite sex!

Pressure was applied to restrict the use of the Indian languages and the children were punished if they were caught speaking their native tongue. Although this was common policy in Indian education, it was seen as a necessity at St. Joseph's because as Shuswap, Carrier, and Chilcotin attended the Mission, it would have been impossible (even if it had been deemed necessary) to provide teachers who could understand and teach in all three dialects. The policy meant little to the children who took the opportunity to speak in their own language when out on walks or in the playground, "as long as a Sister was not around."[16] Father Boening was apparently sympathetic to the Indians' need to talk in their own language as, according to some Alkali Lake Indians, he would speak to them in Shuswap. The Sisters were less flexible. "We use to wonder," said one former pupil, "why they didn't allow us our own language and then they talked in French. It's what I told one of them and they punished me." Yet the Indians laughed at the perplexity of the Sisters when they heard the Indians talking among themselves; "they wondered what we were saying. They thought we were talking about them."

The restrictions imposed on children accustomed to freedom led to frequent desertions. The Indians were not the first children to run away from St. Joseph's, for in the 1870's Father McGuckin complained that white and Métis boys under his care ran away. They too, before the arrival of the Oblates, had become accustomed to a free existence. However, the Indians surpassed them both in quantity and consistency. In September 1901, Father Thomas wrote to Father LeJeune that 48 students had run away during the summer, among them several who had run away two or three times.[17] Unfortunately the children did not always run away in the relatively danger-free summer months. In 1902, Duncan Stick, an eight-year-old boy from Alkali Lake who was among a group of winter-time runaways, died of exposure. By 1910, the problem of runaways was so acute that Father Boening was unable to send any Indian boys out on the farm for instruction.

The reasons given by the children for their constant efforts to escape the school were varied. Some complained of being strapped for such offences as "concealing bedwetting, impertinent language, fighting, and not knowing their lessons"; others wanted freedom from the rigid order of the school; a few girls ran away so that they could "play with the boys"; older boys left because they wanted to work "and earn some money"; many wanted to visit the local rodeos. Occasionally the children gave mystical reasons; for example, two Indian boys told the Sisters that they had left the school because the owl commanded them to do so.[18] Many left for a more prosaic reason: they simply followed the lead of others. As one Indian put it, "I was asked to go and I said O.K." One of the staff remembered, "they'd never be so nice as before they would run away. Sometimes when they'd be extra nice we'd say 'something's going to happen' and sure enough there'd be two or three gone."[19]

Commenting on the runaway situation, Bishop Dontenwill, in an ethnocentric statement, pin-pointed what he felt was responsible. He maintained that while the Mission was endeavouring "to inculcate the principles of religion and morality," the children found moral direction "irksome." The Indians had a "holy horror" of everything which was systemized. When the children had to "face the necessity of going against their hereditary inclinations to indulge in their love for independence and were constrained in their habits of disorder, it was not surprising that they should wish to throw off the yoke of discipline." The Bishop complained that parents and relatives were "abbettors of the truancy," and the support adult Indians gave to the runaways prompted the children "to launch forth with more vigor."

Although compelled by law to send their children to school, many Indian parents resisted. The number attending the Mission rose steadily — by 1907 there were 76 pupils, by 1915 85 attended — yet the number was far less than it should have been, given the geographical area the school covered. The Oblates blamed the ignorance of the parents regarding the advantages of the school and pressed the government to inform the Indians of the Mission's "necessity and benefits to them." Over the years, most Indians came to accept the reality of the Mission School but, as might be expected, the Chilcotin continued to resist.

When the Mission school opened, only one or two Chilcotin attended and they did not remain very long. There was of course the natural problem of distance. The children would have been too far away to allow their parents to visit them. Even the Shuswap and Carrier who lived much closer could not visit as often as they wished to. Many Indians in the Chilcotin country still lived primarily by hunting and trapping, remaining relatively aloof from white contact, and they could easily avoid sending their children away. Father Thomas, who had successfully used his powers of persuasion to good effect among other Indians, could not gain the Chilcotins' acceptance of the school. Added to their obvious distrust of anything white society had to offer, the Chilcotin were opposed also to their children mixing with the children of their traditional enemy.

An Irish nun, Sister Patricia, the first English-speaking Sister of the Child Jesus to come to British Columbia, went to St. Joseph's in 1918. By that time there were about six or seven Chilcotin at the Mission. Sister Patricia recalled:[20]

They were very intelligent the Chilcotin. But I don't think they were ready for school at that time. They're a different type of people altogether than the Shuswap. They liked better to keep on their own. They didn't want to mix up with others. The children were the same. They had their own group.

This aloofness, which Sister Patricia attributed to Chilcotin nature, was partly a resistance to mixing with the Shuswap. Other staff noticed the reluctance of the Chilcotin to mix and Father Alex Morris, school principal between 1946 and 1952, tells one highly illustrative story of how, despite other changes in Indian society, the Chilcotin remained conscious of traditional emnity.[21] When speaking with several boys, the priest had reason to refer to them as Indians.

"Me Chilcotin," asserted one small boy.

"Yes but you are Indian," Father Morris assured him.

"Him an Indian?" queried the boy pointing to a Shuswap.

"Yes," replied the priest.

"Him an Indian, *me* Chilcotin."

The boy was not "being smart." He simply could not conceive of being the same as a Shuswap. Either unaware of or disregarding such strong antipathy, the Oblates and the government agents pressed on with plans to get the Chilcotin to the Mission.

In 1925, R. H. Cairns, federal school inspector, recommended to the Superintendent of Indian education in Ottawa that the Mission be enlarged to accommodate the Chilcotin children. The Pacific Great Eastern Railway now ran through Chilcotin country and, as there was a railway station at the Mission (which was used for shipping Mission stock), the train would provide transportation facilities for the children. There was now no apparent reason why the Chilcotin could not attend the Mission. Several did in fact attend in 1925, but because two children at the Mission died of tuberculosis the Chilcotin parents withdrew them.[22]

Four years later three returned to the school and, in 1932, twelve enrolled. By this time the theory of the Oblates and government agents was that language difficulty might be a reason for slow Chilcotin enrolment. The twelve children however dispelled the fear of local Indian agent H. E. Taylor and the Mission staff that they would have difficulty mixing with other children because of the language barrier; the newcomers were praised as being "most adaptable." Taylor was now optimistic that more would follow and he twice requested that buildings be added to the school to facilitate them. He explained to Ottawa:

> I am receiving continual application from Chilcotin Indians, for admission of their children to school and I feel that we are losing a great opportunity, especially after having overcome the original reluctance of the Chilcotin to make use of the School. If we continually refuse admission to their children the parents will doubtless give up the idea.

Like the missionaries, the agents were given to optimistic statements regarding the Chilcotin; they also suffered the same disappointments. In his Report of 1931 George S. Pragnell, Inspector of Indian Agencies, noted that although some Chilcotin children were being accommodated, "more should be at the school."

By 1932 there were 120 children at the Mission, 34 of whom were Chilcotin. Father George Forbes, school principal, believed the Indians were now "well-disposed" towards the Mission and he was particularly pleased by the presence of the Chilcotin children. He maintained that the progress of the few Chilcotin who had attended in the past despite "general opposition" (presumably from other Chilcotin) had helped to influence others. Three years later, Father Forbes informed the department that he had more applications for admission than he would be able to handle, a situation which proved to the Oblates that both Shuswap and Chilcotin parents were satisfied with the school.

The developing interest of the Chilcotin and the increase in applications from all the Indian groups could have represented a more positive attitude on the part of Indian parents towards the Mission. The Indians of Cariboo may have decided that education was, in the words of Sitting Bull, "something good in the white man's road"[23] and acted accordingly. There is some evidence for this in that the Chilcotin sent their children to school just long enough for them to learn to read and write basic English, make their first Holy Communion, and be Confirmed, and then removed them.[24] Also, in 1932, they requested the Oblates to establish a day school "in their own country," a request that showed an encouraging attitude towards education, as well as the obvious desire to be exclusive.

A letter written in March 1936 gives some insight into another possible explanation for the changing attitude. A Chilcotin wrote to his son at the Mission: "I didn't make much money this year, just enough to buy grub to live on. You are lucky to be in school where you get plenty to eat. If you were home you would get hungry many days." The increase in applications coincided with the Depression years and many Indians were affected by the poor economic situation. Indians may have had to overcome their resistance to the school because the Mission could take care of their children while they searched for work.

Over the years, in spite of constant battles with Ottawa over funds, conditions for the children had improved. Although the staff enforced a rigid routine, they increased and expanded recreational activities. In the early days the children had made their own amusements, and walks in the surrounding area were the only organized recreation. By 1929, school concerts had become part of the curriculum. The children made the costumes, scenery and decorations. They were "wonderfully artistic" and at the Kamloops fair in 1932 boys from the Mission took first prize in agriculture, and the girls took second prize in needlework and painting and third prize in cooking.

The Oblates expanded the school manual training facilities and, according to the Indian agent, the boys received "invaluable training in the operation of machinery and the conducting of ranch activities." This was a far cry from the days when, during his years at the Mission, David Johnson learned by trial and error how to cobble shoes. The Mission employed some of the boys on the ranch during the summer months and every year the girls' graduating class spent the summer picking and canning the many fruits and vegetables grown at the Mission. But this program of part academic, part practical training was drawing to a close. The Mission was heading towards a period of change.

NOTES TO CHAPTER VIII

[1] Unless otherwise stated, all quoted material in this chapter is taken from the R.G. 10 files, Volumes: 6436; 6437; 6438; 6811.

[2] Robert Berkhofer Jr., "Model Zions for the American Indians," *American Quarterly*, Vol. 15, 1963, p. 177.

[3] Ronald N. Satz, *American Indian Policy in the Jacksonian Era*, Lincoln, Nebraska, 1975, p. 248.

[4] Elizabeth Graham, *Medicine Man to Missionary: Missionaries as Agents of Change among the Indians of Southern Ontario*, Toronto, 1975, p. 65.

[5] This view was held by the Oblates as late as 1957.

[6] Sister Marie Anne of Jesus, Superior, to Bishop D'herbomez, May 23, 1888, A.S.S.A., Victoria.

[7] Paul Durieu to Sister Marie de la Providence, April 15, 1890, A.S.S.A. Victoria.

[8] Minutes of the Oblate Vicariate Council Meeting, November 12, 1891, File No. P.B.517, A.D.

[9] Minutes of the Oblate Vicariate Council Meeting, November 22, 1893, File No. P.B.517, A.D.

[10] Minutes of the Oblate Vicariate Council Meeting, October 6, 1894, File No. P.B.517, A.D.

[11] Sister Jean Gabriel, S.C.J., Provincial Superior North Battleford, Saskatchewan, to Sister Mary Theodore, S.S.A., August 11, 1943, A.S.S.A. Victoria.

[12] P. Coron, S.J. *Messengers of the Holy City*, Lyon, France, 1969, pp. 146-148.

[13] Father Thomas to Father Forbes, date unknown, O.A.

[14] John F. Bryde, *Modern Indian Psychology*, South Dakota, 1971, p. 96.

[15] Interview with Alkali Lake Indians.

[16] Interview with Sister Patricia, S.C.J. (Cited hereafter as Sister Patricia, S.C.J.)

[17] Father Thomas to Father LeJeune, September 23, 1901, A.D.

[18] Sister Patricia, S.C.J.

[19] *Ibid.*

[20] *Ibid.*

[21] Interview with Father Alex Morris, O.M.I., August 30, 1980. (Cited hereafter as Alex Morris, O.M.I.)

[22] Interview with Father John Hennessy, O.M.I., March 8, 1979.

[23] Bryde, *Modern Indian Psychology*, p. 11.

[24] Alex Morris, O.M.I.

Chapter IX

A NEW ERA

The 1940's brought significant changes to the Mission. Father Thomas still travelled from reserve to reserve, preaching through an interpreter, presiding at "courts," always on schedule, seemingly tireless in his efforts to bring religion to the Indians. Until 1936, with the exception of one or two temporary helpers, he had worked alone, and undoubtedly he would have preferred to continue that way. But the French missionary was now turned sixty and the Oblate Council decided that he must have a permanent assistant. In 1936, Vancouver-born Father John Hennessy arrived at St. Joseph's. He was the first English-speaking missionary in the Cariboo since the days of Father McGuckin.

For the first time in forty years, the Oblates divided the mission territory and Father Hennessy took over the Chilcotin country. The Indians now had a priest who could converse with them in English, but to their request that he abandon the use of the interpreter system and preach in English, the new missionary said no. Father Thomas still held sway, and he trained Father Hennessy the way Bishop Durieu trained him. However, the English missionary visited the Chilcotin on a more regular basis, at least eight visits a year, a definite deviation from Father Thomas's pattern. This did not come about without protest from the "elder statesman" who, unlike those involved in Indian education, was convinced that it was not in the Indians' nature to keep to a regular routine and that consequently his three or four visits a year on special feast days was more acceptable to them.[1]

Despite Father Thomas's insistence on its form, the Durieu System was weakening. The Mission school was partly responsible, for the children, taught their religion in the conventional Catholic mode, grew up impatient of a system that was becoming alien to them. The Indians' request to Father Hennessy was indicative of their changing attitude. The missionaries also came to regard the system as outmoded. Other missionaries arrived at St. Joseph's whose outlook was totally at variance with that of Father Thomas. One of them, Father Alex Morris from the Gaspé coast, Quebec, recorded how he ignored the interpreters and began preaching to the Shuswap in English, a situation which earned him the displeasure of Father Thomas but the gratitude of the Indians[2] (with the possible exception of the now defunct interpreters).

The "court system" lingered on into the forties in some areas, but as the chiefs lost a lot of their authority it too came to an end. Indian Agent Bill Christie recalled his own participation in one of the last Durieu courts held at Redstone. In the absence of the missionary, Mr. Christie, who as a J.P. had legal authority, presided at a court held in front of the church. Indians who had caused harm while drunk had to kneel in front of the Chief and Mr. Christie while their crimes were assessed. The Chief levied fines against those found guilty and, Mr. Christie recalled, "if they didn't pay, they'd take a horse or cow and sell it and the money went to the church, to buy candles and stuff like that."[3] Even without church or government authority present, one or two chiefs continued to hold these courts but the Indians refused to participate; in one case, where the Chief had taken a man's horse because of nonpayment of a fine, the Indian reported it to the R.C.M.P. — a sure sign of the loss of tribal and Church authority.

Father Thomas, who died in 1957, attempted to keep the system alive until poor health forced his retirement from missionary work. Most Oblates were happy to see the passing of the system but some regarded its passing with regret. At Father Thomas's funeral, Brother Patrick Collins who had spent many years working at St. Joseph's remarked: "It is noticeable that since his method of teaching religion has been stopped, piety and Church ruling has not been going on so well and it is feared that if such a way is let go on a few more years, prayer and religion will be lost altogether."[4] While his missionary method disappeared, another of Paul Durieu's plans for St. Joseph's was revived.

On December 8, 1947, the first six postulants of the newly created all-Indian Sisterhood of Mary Immaculate began their religious life in a novitiate at the Chilcotin Anaham Reserve. The order was placed under the guidance of Father Francis Sutherland O.M.I. and the young girls who came from reserves throughout British Columbia were trained by Sisters of Christ the King. Other girls joined the original group but, like its predecessor, the novitiate failed. While their intentions were good, the young Indian girls lacked perseverance. According to Mother St. Paul who was the Superior at Anaham, the girls loved their freedom too much and they seldom stayed longer than a year or two. Only two completed their training at Anaham and the novitiate closed in the late 1950's.[5]

The presence of the Sisters of Christ the King among the Chilcotin represented another change in St. Joseph's Mission district. The Oblates lost their autonomous position in the early 1900's. The province had secular clergy as well as missionaries and, as history repeated itself, the two sometimes clashed. In the 1940's, Archbishop Duke of Vancouver, or the "Iron Duke" as he was often called, was frequently at odds with the Oblates. One major area of contention was the Oblate preference for the Mission school over day schools on the reserves. By 1941, two day schools were operating in St. Joseph's Mission district. The Elgatcho Indians had a day school which the Indians had built; the Chief "had put a teacher in it himself."[6] The Redstone Indians had a partial school. In spring, the Redstone children went hunting and trapping with their parents and they worked on the land during summer and fall. Father Hennessy held school in the church building from the end of October until March, during which time he had complete care of the children. Archbishop Duke favoured regular day schools on other reserves and the Oblates favoured continuation of the Mission school. The Archbishop, with the willing help of Bill Christie, who saw in day schools encouragement for the Indians to settle, persuaded Ottawa to finance regular day schools at Anaham and Redstone. The "Iron Duke" persuaded the Sisters of Christ the King to come to British Columbia to work in the new schools. The Mission school however continued to be the major educator for the Cariboo's children.

In spite of the efforts of more enlightened and lenient Oblates and Sisters to make learning less arduous and to provide recreational outlets for the children's energy, the children continued to run away from the school. The hiring of a night watchman as a fire precaution hindered would-be escapees for a while but determination prevailed; in 1943, the agent reported that a number of Alkali Lake boys "broke away from the School and were two nights camped out in the bush." The following year, the principal, Father McGrath, made the children happier by such innovations as a "magic lantern slide show" and by giving them "more freedom and less discipline." Bill Christie was delighted to report to Ottawa that the boys particularly were afforded more liberty of movement and consequently there were fewer truancies. Unfortunately this state of affairs was brief. A month later, in spite of Mr. Christie's optimism, 23 boys ran away to go to the Alkali Lake stampede.[7] The agent had to demand that the Oblates engage a disciplinarian or he would be forced to shut down the school.

In 1946, the appointment of a new principal brought important fundamental changes. As soon as he took over the school, Father Alex Morris made a psychologically important change. He insisted that French was not to be spoken at all, at any time, in the presence of Indian children. Any French Sisters who addressed him in French would be translated and answered in English.[8] A small injustice but an important one had been put to right. Of greater importance, the Mission moved from the half-day academic, half-day practical work programme to the full British Columbia school curriculum. Both Father Morris and Father Bert Dunlop, who was principal at Sechelt Residential School, believed the time had come for the Indian children to be integrated into the regular school system. With help from the school personnel in Williams Lake, the necessary changes were made. The boys continued to learn agricultural pursuits but in a more enjoyable way. The school started a Calf Club which was under the direction of Mr. Christie and Jack McCluckie, the Mission foreman, both experienced men. In this way, the children learned more scientific husbandry. Father Morris was also concerned with the lack of what he considered "an essential element," that of music. The school hired piano and organ teachers, and the Indian boys whom a year earlier had formed a squadron of Air Force Cadets, were encouraged to participate in a pipe and drum band. "We had no Indian music," declared Father Morris, "so I introduced the music we had."

Following the dictum that any music was valuable, the new principal, together with the commanding officer of the boys' squadron, planned musical involvement for the girls. Hoping to get local financial support, the two men decided to persuade the government to purchase the instruments of an East Kootenay bagpipe band, so that they could form a girls' pipe band. Urged on by enthusiastic support from Bill Christie — understandable as he was a Scot — the government purchased the instruments and the young girls quickly formed a creditable band. Although he later came under attack for involving the girls in something so alien to their culture, Father Morris did not regret his actions; "my basic purpose was that they learn music; music, any music, was essential." In making his changes, the principal met only once with resistance from the Indians. Father Morris had observed that the poor handling of furs was cutting into some Indians' profits. In order to remedy this, he hired an experienced man to teach the Indian children how to cure fur pelts correctly. The Indians opposed the move and the lessons ended. The other changes met with unqualified approval and there was one obvious, positive result from the new policies. Between 1946 and 1952 only one child, a girl, ran away from the Mission — and she was found sleeping under a tree near the Sugar Cane Reserve.

Capitalizing on growing parent interest, the Mission Oblates together with the Indian agent attempted to introduce an adult, two week, "Pro-Recreation" programme at the school. Chief David Johnson, Tommy Harry, May and Augusta Johnson, all from Alkali Lake, attended the course. As a result, the Chief decided to have a building erected on the reserve for recreational purposes. Mr. Christie admitted however that the programme had limited success. It was difficult to raise Indian interest in a recreational programme when most of them "were out working."

While the staff were making adjustments at the Mission, external events foreshadowed the end of denominational control of Indian education, and the end of an era at St. Joseph's. Following the advice of Indian witnesses, a Special Joint Committee of the Senate and the House of Commons recommended that the federal government should exercise its responsibility for Indian education. The committee acknowledged that the Indians declared themselves grateful for the part of the Churches in financing their education but they now desired complete government control. Because it was "an extremely difficult task" to provide an educational programme for the children of Indians who were still engaged in hunting, trapping and other seasonal activities over a large area, the committee concluded that residential schools should be maintained for pupils not within range of day schools. Wherever possible, however, the day-school system had to be inaugurated and day schools established on the reserves. Consequently, by 1957, several day schools had been established among the Shuswap, Carrier, and Chilcotin. In spite of this, the Mission remained the Cariboo Indians' primary education centre. In 1957, for example, a total of 41 Shuswap children attended three day schools, while 154 Shuswap attended the Mission. The Oblates continued to operate the school until 1964 when the federal government took complete control.

Many of the older generation look back on their days at the Mission with a certain affection. They agree that things were tough, but they remember the fun times too. Their feelings regarding the Mission might well be reflected in the words of Bud Felker who attended the school in the early 1900's: "I tell you, no fooling, it was a pretty good school. . . . I meet some of the Indian men who went to school with me and they say 'Not too bad a place that Mission school.' "[9] The younger generation, or many of them, would not agree. They resent the part played by the Mission in undermining their cultural heritage.

Although no longer involved in education, the Oblates remain in Cariboo to continue over one hundred years of ministry to the Indian peoples. Three Oblate priests now cover an area once covered singlehandedly by Father Thomas; a fourth, from Fort St. James, flies in to visit Anaham Lake and the Elgatcho Indians. The Mission ranch, pride of Father McGuckin, is now in other hands; but its sale will benefit numerous Oblate missions. "The Mission," as everyone in Cariboo knew it, has gone; but its history remains a rich part of Cariboo heritage.

NOTES TO CHAPTER IX

1 Interview with Father John Hennessy, June 19, 1980.

2 Alex Morris, O.M.I.

3 Interview with William (Bill) Christie, June 6, 1980. (Cited hereafter as Mr. Christie.)

4 Brother Patrick Collins, O.M.I. Manuscript, O.A.

5 Interview with Mother St. Paul, April 5, 1979.

6 Mr. Christie.

7 *Ibid.*

8 Alex Morris, O.M.I.

9 "Rapping with Bud," Uncatalogued undated manuscript, St. Joseph's Mission, Williams Lake.

INDEX

Accolti, S. J., Father Michael, 15
Ahtanum, 16
Alachicas, 16
Alaska, 13, 32
Alderville, 110
Alexandria, 28, 48, 104
  Indians of, 47, 81, 83, 89, 91
  see also Fort Alexandria
Alexis, Chief (Chilcotin), 52
Alexis Creek, 105
  Indians of, 105
Alkali Lake, 35, 45, 48, 81, 121, 132-34
  Indians of, 35, 82, 90, 94, 104, 123, 124
  stampede, 133
American Presbyterian General Assembly, 109-10
Anaham, 100, 104, 105, 131-32
  people of, 100, 102, 104, 135
  Anaham Lake, 135
Anaham, Chief (Chilcotin), 52, 99
Annette, 102
Arles, 12
Ashcroft, 117
Athapascan Indians, 27

Babines, 27, 58
Barkerville, 37, 41, 69
Barnard, Francis James, M.P., 109, 119-20
Bates, Mr., 61, 64, 91
Baudre, Father Julien, 44
Beaver, Reverend Herbert, 15
Begbie, Judge Matthew Baillie, 61, 62, 96
Bell (Indian Agent), 120
Belleau, David, 123
Beni, Indian prophet, 32
Bermond, Father François, 20
Blanchet, Archbishop Francis Norbert, 15, 17, 18, 22, 74
  as missionary priest, 13-14
Blanchet, Bishop Magloire, 15-17, 22
Blanchet, Brother Georges, 11, 47-49, 55, 80
  as priest, 80-81
Boening, Father Heinrich, 119, 124
Bolduc, Father, J. B., 15
Borland Creek, 91
Boston Bar, 88
Bourget, Bishop Ignace, 12-13
Bridges, Mr., 119, 121
Brittany, 97, 98
Brophy, Mr., 119
Buckland, Frank, 55
Bunoz, Bishop Emile, 98, 104

Cache Creek, 71
  school, 73-74
Cairns, R. H., 126
Calhoun, John C., 110
California, 21, 42, 112
Cambrian Hall, 37
Cameron, John, 41
Cameronton, 41
Canim Lake, 27, 103
  Indians of, 103
Canoe Creek, 48, 81, 102-03
  Indians of, 82, 88
Canon Law, 16
Captain Bobby, 104
Carew-Gibson, E. A., 121
Cariboo, 9, 23, 34-37, 41, 42, 44, 57, 63, 71-73, 77, 80, 88, 95, 109, 135
  Indians of, 27-29, 79, 80, 89, 93, 98, 101, 104, 109, 113, 127
  Residential School, 9, 109, 119
Carrier Indians, 27-29, 31-35, 46-48, 50, 81, 104, 123, 134

Catholic Ladder, 18, 22
  invented, 14
Cariboo Sentinel, 70
Cayuse Indians, 15, 55
Chiappini, Father Jean Dominic, 100
Chilcotin, 36, 50, 81, 98, 130, 131
  Indians of, 27-29, 34-36, 46-47, 51-52, 83-84, 87, 98, 102, 104, 123, 125-27, 134
  River, 27
  see also Fort Chilcotin
Chimney Creek, 35
  Indians of, 35, 82
Chinese, 42, 63, 67
Chirouse, Father Casimir, 11, 103
Chirouse Jr., Father Casimir, 96-97
Christie, William (Bill), Indian Agent, 131-34
Clerics of St. Viator, 21
Clinton, 27, 48, 69, 96
Common Schools, 69, 71-72, 74
  missionaries attitude towards, 67-69, 73, 74, 77
Collegiate School, 67
Columbia River, 28
Colville, 15
Cooleystown, 43
Council of the Sisters of St. Ann, 71
Council of the Vicariate, 69, 116
  see also Oblate Council; Provincial Council
County Tyrone, 43
Cowichan Indians, 21
Cox, Judge William, 52
Coyote, 29-30
Cranbrook, 111

Daily British Colonist, 90
Davie, Alexander, E. B., 62
Davison, R. V., 120
Daunt (Indian Agent), 122
Deep Creek, 45, 91
De Mazenod, Bishop Eugene, 11-13, 18, 20-22, 43, 84, 85
Demers, Bishop Modeste, 15, 20-22
  as missionary, 13-14, 34-35
Department of Indian Affairs, 111, 112
De Smet, S. J., Father Peter John, 14, 15
D'herbomez, Bishop Louis, 22, 23, 36, 42, 44-48, 53, 55, 56, 59, 66-72, 74, 76, 79-80, 84, 86, 88, 91
  as missionary, 16, 20, 21
  death of, 94

Dick, Amelia, 123
Dog Creek, 48
  Indians of, 82
Dontenwill, Bishop Augustine, 103, 125
Dublin, 43
Duke, Archbishop William Mark, 132
Duncan, Wlliam, 49
Dunlevy, Mr., 70
Dunlop, Father Herbert, 133
Durieu, Bishop Paul, 71, 86, 93, 97, 106, 109-19
  as missionary, 16, 17, 54, 58, 59, 66, 87
  death of, 103
  see also Durieu System
Durieu System, 18, 52, 94-95, 96-97, 99
  explanations of, 18-19, 51, 101
  Indian attitude towards, 23, 47, 81, 94, 100, 130-31
  missionary attitude towards, 49, 98, 131
  demise of in Cariboo, 130-31

Eagle, Charles, 77
East Kootenay, 133
Elgatcho Indians, 98, 99, 135
  reserve, 104
Episcopal Church, 43
Esquimalt, 21
Evans, Reverend Doctor, 43
Europe, 122
Egypt Reserve, 104

Fabre, Father Joseph, 22, 23
Fagnant, Mr., 14
Fahy, Mr., 119
Felker, Bud, 135
  family, 44, 46, 73
  farm, 63
Flathead Indians, 14
Forbes, Father George, 127
Fort Alexandria, 28, 34, 35, 46, 51, 83
Fort Chilcotin, 29, 34
Fort Douglas, 22
Fort George, 27, 28
Fort Kluskus, 29, 99
Fort Okanagan, 34
Fort Rupert, 21
Fort Simpson, 49
Fort St. James, 27, 32
Fort Thompson, 28, 34
Fort Vancouver, 13, 15, 28
Foster, Dr., 96

Fouquet, Father Leon, 21-22, 44
Fraser River, 22, 98, 100
Fraser, Simon, 27
French Revolution, 11

Gaspé, Quebec, 131
Gendre, Father Florimund, 44
General Chapter of the Oblates, 71
Government
  Federal, 87-89, 105, 112, 116, 133-34
  Provincial, 87
  attitude to Indians, 87, 91, 96
Gragheald, 74
Graham ranch, 59, 63
Grandidier, Father Charles, 22, 45, 84
Grouse Creek, 42
Guertin, Father Frederick, 86
Guichon, Lawrence, 92
Gulf of St. Lawrence, 13

Hanley, Michael, 77
Harmon, Danial, 31, 34
Hennessy, Father John (Jack), 130, 132
Hill, Anglican Bishop George, 23, 67
Holy Rosary parish, 98
Hope, 22
Horan, Mr., 115
Horris, Father Edward, 51, 62
Howe, Oliver, 62
Hudson's Bay Company, 15, 28, 47

Inchicore, 43
Indian churches and chapels:
  L'Assomption, Clinton, 48
  Sainte Anne, Soda Creek, 48
  Saint Gabriel, Canoe Creek, 48
  Saint Jacques, Alexandria, 48
  Saint John's, Kluskus, 105
  Saint Laurent, Tli-te-Naitan, 48
  Sainte Marie Refuge des Pécheurs, 48
  Saint Michael, Quesnel, 48
  Saint Paul, Dog Creek, 48
  Saint Paul, Quesnel, 48
  Saint Pierre, Alkali Lake, 48
Indian novitiate, 118, 131
Indian parlour, 123
Indian Total Abstinence Society, 95
Indian Chiefs, *see* individual listing
Indians, tribes and bands, *see* individual listing
Interior Salish, 27
Ireland, 12, 43, 74
Iroquois Indians, 33

Jacquet, Peter, 14
Jameson, Reverend R., 66
Janin, Brother Gaspard, 16, 21
Jayol, Father Francis, 45, 46, 48
Jenness, Diamond, 33
Jesuit missionaries, *see* individual listing
Johnson, Augusta, 134
Johnson, Celestine, 123
Johnson, David, 123, 128, 134
Johnson, May, 134

Kamiakin, Chief (Yakima), 16
Kamloops, 28, 34, 65, 80, 93
  Kamloops Indian Residential School, 111, 113
Kelly, Mr., 90
Keogh, Chief (Chilcotin), 52
Kerwin, Patrick, 41-44
Kilapoutkue, Chief (Lillooets), 96
Klatsassen, Chief (Chilcotin), 35
Kluskus, 29
  Indians of, 99, 103, 105
  Lake, 83, 104
  see also Fort Kluskus
Kra-al, Baptiste, 90
Kwakiutl Indians, 21, 49

Lachine, 70, 71
Lac La Hache, 77
Lallier, Monsieur, 41, 67
Langlois, Father A., 15
Lapierre, Baptiste, 29
Lee, Norman, 100
Lee, Sheriff, 67
LeJacq, Father Jean Marie, 44, 47-50, 51, 57-59, 75, 80, 81, 83-85, 96, 113, 116, 119
LeJeune, Father Jean Marie, 93, 94, 103, 124
Lemdrum, Tommy, 104
Lemmens, Bishop John Nicholas, 94
Lenihan, James, Indian Commissioner, 88-90, 92
Le Puy, France, 114, 117
Liege, Belgium, 98
Lillooet, 80, 89, 98
  Indians of, 81, 96
Lower Richfield, 41
  see also Barkerville
Lundin-Brown, Reverend, R-C., 35
Lytton, 80

MacCarril, Patrick, 115
Mackay, D. J., 105
Manitoba, 32

Marchal, Father Charles, 61, 62, 75, 81-83, 85-87, 90, 93
Marseilles, 13, 43, 84
McBean, William, 33-34
McBride, James, 77
McCluckie, John (Jack), 133
McGrath, Father James, 132
McGuckin, Father James Maria, 41-54, 56-65, 66-70, 72-77, 79-92, 105, 124
McIlveen, James, 67
McKenzie, Alexander, 27
McKinley, James, 90
McLean, John, 32
McLeod Lake, 27
Meason, William L., 111
Messier, Mr., 62
Methodist missionaries, 13
Methodist or Presbyterian Society of Ontario, 91
Métis, 77, 103, 124
Miners, 21, 42, 44, 50, 58
Minor Seminaries, 21, 53
Mission City, 22
Missionaries: and Indian rights, 87-92, 100, 105
  difficulties of, 13, 16, 17, 20, 23, 53, 72-74, 81, 115-16, 120-21
  Indian response to, 11, 14, 35-36, 47, 48, 51-52, 81-84, 94, 99, 100, 123-25, 127, 131
Missionary Society of Provence, 11
Missouri, 17
Montreal, 12-13, 110, 117
Mother Alphonsine, S. C. J., 114
Mother Mary Eulalie, S.S.A., 70, 75
Mother St. Paul, S.C.K., 132
Morice, Father Adrian, 33, 82, 100
Morris, Father Alex, 131, 133, 134
Muncey, 110
Murphy, Dennis, 44, 45, 62, 70
Murphy, William, 77
Musgrave, Governor Anthony, 69

Napoleon, 11
Nechako River, 27
New Caledonia, 15, 20
New Westminster, 22, 48, 53, 57, 66, 67, 68, 71, 77, 91, 94, 98
New York, 117
Nisqually, 15, 20
Nobili, Father John, S. J., 15, 35, 36
North Battleford, 119
North Vancouver, 98

Oblate Constitution and Rules, 13, 18, 21, 53, 84
Oblate Council, 20, 56
Oblate missions
  Oregon Territory: Immaculate Conception, 16
  St. Joseph's of Simcoe, 16
  St. Joseph's Olympia, 16, 22
  St. Rose, 11, 15
  British Columbia: Okanagan, 21, 55, 60
  Our Lady of Good Hope, 27, 80
  St. Charles, New Westminster, 22
  St. Joseph's, Williams Lake, 9, 45-48, 50-51, 53, 55, 57, 58, 64-65, 66-69, 71, 73-82, 85-86, 88-89, 91, 93, 94, 97, 103, 109, 112-13, 124, 125, 131, 134
  St. Louis, Kamloops, 65
  St. Mary's, Mission City, 22, 53, 67, 111
  St. Michael's Fort Rupert, 21
Oblate novitiate, 98
Oblates of Mary Immaculate
  founded in, 11
  original purpose, 11-12
  begin foreign mission work, 12
  in Canada, 13
  in Oregon, 11
  in British Columbia, 21
Oblate Procurator, 58
Ogden, Peter Skene, 28
Okanagan Valley, 21
Olympia, 16, 17, 19, 20
Omineca, 58
Ootsa Lake, 99
Oppenheimer, brothers, 62
  David, 62
Ontario, 110
Orange Order, 68
Oregon City, 15
Oregon Missions, 11, 16
  end of, 21
  see also individual listings
Oregon Territory, 11, 13, 15
O'Reilly, Peter, 99
Ottawa, 114, 119-21, 126-28, 133

Pacific Great Eastern Railway, 126
Pandosy, Father Charles John Felix, 11, 19, 21
Papineau Rebellion, 15
Paris, 71
Petiteau, Mme., 73

Piopiomosmos, Chief (Walla Walla), 11
Pomeroy, Mr., 45
farm/ranch, 45, 56
Pope Leo XII, 12
Potlatch, 93-94
Powell, Dr. Israel Wood, 87-89
Pragnell, George S., 127
Presbyterian missions, 15
missionaries, *see* individual listing
minister, 66
Prophet Movement, 32
Provence, 11
Provincial Council, 75
Puget Sound, Indians of, 16, 19

Quebec, 49, 70, 75
diocese of, 13
Bishop of, 13
Queen Charlotte Islands, 13, 49
Quesnel, 45, 48, 61, 62, 81, 86, 103, 104
Indians of, 89
Quesnelmouth, 44

Ravalli, S. J., Father Anthony, 15
Red River, 13
Redstone, 105, 131
Indians of, 131, 132
Redstone Plateau, 105
Report of the Vicariate of British Columbia, 65
Ricard, Father Pascal, 11, 19
Richard, Father Pierre, 16, 21
Richfield, town of, 41-44, 48, 58, 68
parish of, 44, 48, 58, 81
Rocky Mountains, 13
Rocky Point, 63
Royal Canadian Mounted Police, 131
Ryerson, Dr. Egerton, 110

Saanich Indians, 21
Sacred Propoganda in Rome, 16
Sahale Stick, 14
Sam, Chief (Carrier), 4
San José River Valley, 45
River, 50, 56, 90
Valley, 9
Saskatchewan, 119
Sawyer, John, 62
Scott, M. (Indian Superintendent), 120
Sechelt, 93-94, 98
Indians of, 93
Sechelt Residential School, 133
Sergeant, Reverend John, 109
Shaman, 19
Shuswap Indians, 27-36, 45, 46, 49, 50, 81, 83, 93, 94, 98, 102 104, 123-27
Shearer, Edward, 60-62
Sheepshanks, Reverend John, 43
Sicklinghall, Yorkshire, 43
Signay, Bishop Joseph, 13
Simpson, Sir George, 15
Sisterhood of Mary Immaculate, 131
Sisters of St. Ann, 53, 67, 70, 72, 74, 75, 112-13, 115-16
at Williams Lake, 64-65, 75-76
at Lachine, 71
in Victoria, 74
see also Council of the Sisters of St. Ann
Sister Marie Clement, S.S.A., 75
Sister Marie Hélène, S.S.A., 75
Sister Marie Joachim, S.S.A., 75
Sister Marie Octavia, S.S.A., 75
Sister Mary Infant Jesus, S.S.A. 75, 78
Sister Mary Providence, S.S.A., 113
Sisters of the Child Jesus, 114, 117
at Williams Lake, 117-19, 124, 125
Sister Aimée de Marie, S.C.J., 117
Sister Euphrasia, S.C.J., 117
Sister Saint-Fabian, S.C.J., 117
Sister Félician, S.C.J., 117-18
Sister Patricia, S.C.J., 125-26
Sisters of Christ the King, 131-32
Sisters of Notre Dame of Namur, 15
Sisters of the Presentation, 74-75
Sisters of Providence (Oregon), 74-75
Sister Peter, S.P., 75
Sitting Bull, 127
Sliammon Mission, 98
Smith, Marcus, 87-88
Society for the Propagation of the Faith, 66
Soda Creek, 35, 45, 48, 50, 72, 81, 89
Indians of 81, 82, 86, 91
Spalding, Reverend Henry, 15
Special Joint Committee of the Senate and the House of Commons, 134
Spokane Gerry, 32
St. Gerlach, 98
Saint Joseph's Mission, Williams Lake, *see* Oblate missions
St. Louis Church, Victoria, 66
St. Louis College, 43, 66, 67

St. Louis, Missouri, 17
St. Joseph's Hospital, Victoria, 75
St. Patrick's Church, 43, 46, 48
parish, 81
Stalo Indians, 118
Stikeen Indians, 50
Stony Indians, 52
Stuart Lake, 27, 35, 47, 58, 73, 80
Sugar Cane Reserve, 91, 95, 102, 104, 134
Indians of, 94
Sulphician Order, 110
Surel, Brother Phillipe, 16, 21, 59
Sutherland, Father Francis, 132

Taylor, H. E. (Indian Agent), 126
Taylor, Reverend Lachler, 43
Tempier, Father François-Henri, 12
Tête Jeune Cache, 33
Thomas, Father François Marie, 50, 83, 97-102, 104-06
Tloos mission, 98
Toomey, Mr., 44, 45
Tougan, 102
Trahillet, Captain, 67
Tréssierra, José, 45
Toronto, 88
Tulalip, 21

Upper Ottawa, 13
Upper Saint-Maurice, 13

Vancouver, 104
Vancouver Island, 15, 21, 53, 94
Vankoughnet, L., 90, 99, 119
Vercruisse, S.J., Father Louis, 15
Verney, Brother Celestine, 11
Vicariate-Apostolic, 15, 20
Vicariate of British Columbia, 22
Victoria, 21, 23, 66, 73, 74, 75, 87, 88, 113
Vijnsko, George, 67
Vowell, A. G. (Indian Superintendent), 99, 111, 113, 115, 120-21

Waddington Massacre, 35
Walla Walla, 11, 15
Walkem, George, 62 96
Waspuilor, William, 103
Water right, 59
Wesleyans, 43
Willamette Valley, 13, 14
William, Chief (Shuswap), 34, 35, 81-82
Williams Creek, 41, 44
Williams Lake, 9, 50, 133
Wright, Dr., 105